Christiantown, USA

Christiantown, USA

Richard Stellway

The Haworth Press
New York • London

85924

Christiantown, USA is Volume Number 1 in the Haworth Series in Marriage and the Family.

The Haworth Press, Inc. 10 Alice Street, Binghamton, NY 13904-1580
EUROSPAN/Haworth, 3 Henrietta Street, London WC2E 8LU England

Library of Congress Cataloging-in-Publication Data

Stellway, Richard J., 1943 –
    Christiantown, U.S.A. / Richard Stellway.
        p.   cm. – (Haworth series in marriage and family ; v. no. 1)
    Includes bibliographical references.
    ISBN 0-86656-903-0 (alk. paper) : ISBN 0-86656-908-1
(pbk. : alk. paper) :
    1. Family – United States. 2. Family – Religious life – United States. I. Title. II. Series.
HQ536.S763   1990
306.85 – dc20   90-33833
                                                                                        CIP

In Loving Memory of

Fritz Fliegel

A professor who helped to instill in me a respect for the research craft and
its contribution to human understanding.

CONTENTS

ABOUT THE AUTHOR

Richard Stellway, PhD, is Professor and Chairperson of the Sociology Department at Northwest Nazarene College in Nampa, Idaho. Prior to joining the faculty there, he taught marriage and family courses at a number of colleges and universities and organized several marriage life conferences and workshops. A member of the National Council on Family Relations, Dr. Stellway is a past President of the affiliated Idaho-Montana Council on Family Relations.

Dr. Stellway has had several overseas educational experiences. He spent 1981 in India as a Fulbright Fellow; 1983 in Costa Rica; and 1985 in Cairo, Egypt as part of the National Council on U.S.-Arab Relations scholar program. Then, as a recipient of a Fulbright-Hayes award, he participated in the "Korea: History & Culture" seminar in Seoul, Korea (1986). During his sabbatical in Kenya (1988) he helped lay the foundation for a study of Kenya youth and, more recently, edited a study of family planning materials in that country.

Editor's Note

One of the most misunderstood groups in America today is also one of the largest: people who identify themselves as Christians. What is particularly enigmatic about this segment of the population is that it represents both a religion and a culture. From the religious perspective, the tenets and beliefs are fairly well understood. However, from a cultural standpoint, little is really known. With the increased media attention being paid to born-again Christians, their newfound entry into the political arena, and the unfortunate misdeeds of some of their most vociferous spokesmen, the televangelists, it is critical that empirical research be conducted so that the true sociology of this highly visible and influential subculture is understood.

This book reports on the first major sociological study of Christian families and family life. Through both quantitative and qualitative research methods, the author provides important empirical data on the behaviors, attitudes, goals, and experiences of a large group of couples from Wheaton, Illinois. Like the classic study of a half century ago, *Middletown, A Study in Contemporary Culture*, this work examines in detail the lives of a random sample of people from one U.S. city. In this case, however, the city was chosen not because of its representativeness of the U.S. in general, but because it uniquely represents a *Christian* community.

Christiantown, USA is not only an academically sound record of the results of this fascinating study, but also is enjoyable to read. This book should prove of interest to sociologists, social workers, psychologists, counselors, and the general public. Most people from both secular and religious backgrounds will find this to be a balanced and unbiased report, although some may find the results controversial, particularly if they have preconceived ideas of what a

Christian family is like or how a Christian family should behave. All, however, should find this book to be an important contribution to the field of family studies.

Terry S. Trepper, PhD, Series Editor
Haworth Series in Marriage and the Family

Foreword

Ernst Troeltsch, in his classic work, *The Social Teaching of the Christian Churches*, identified what he called "The Laxist Tendency." He believed that although most religious groups began with a fervent rejection of the World, over time they almost inevitably become part of the World. Reading Richard Stellway's study of Christiantown, USA, I couldn't help thinking that Troeltsch was right after all. Since this is the first community study of evangelical families, I was expecting to learn how different they are from average American families. But findings on page after page are the same as findings from secular community studies such as *Middletown*. For example, How "Happy" are these couples with their marriages? The response, says Professor Stellway, "comes surprisingly close to the national average." What are their sex lives like? About the same as reported by most married couples. Are their children much different from what we know about children in general? No. And finally the most surprising finding of all: "Christiantowners most conform to the modernist model of marriage. In fact, there is considerable evidence of role flexibility and role sharing."

What to conclude? In terms of the ways in which Professor Stellway conducted his fascinating study, evangelical families are in the mainstream. In Troeltsch's terms, they have become part of the society and culture around them. There may be other, more subtle ways in which evangelical families are different, but it will be up to a later study to show how. In the interim, this book fills a gap in our knowledge about white, middle-class affluent suburbanite evangelicals. And the knowledge is that for all practical purposes, they have acculturated.

John Scanzoni
Professor of Sociology
University of Florida

Preface

While growing up in a rather conservative working-class home and while attending a middle-class Protestant church, I recall various pronouncements being made on the virtues of Christian marriage, the Christian family, and the Christian home. I remember viewing television messages such as "the family that prays together stays together," and reading similar slogans on church bulletin boards. I recall hearing members of the middle-class Protestant church I attended give testimonial accounts of how Christ had made all the difference in their marriages. The message I was picking up was very clear: Christians have good marriages, and non-Christians do not.

There may have been a time when I uncritically acceded to these claims but I do recall struggling with apparent exceptions to the rule. Upon sharing these concerns with other church members, it was suggested to me that these exceptions did not invalidate the rule (namely, that Christianity makes a difference) since those Christians who did have marital problems experienced them because they were not "good" Christians, they failed to pray sufficiently, or they lacked sufficient commitment to God or to the church. This line of logic helped sustain my belief, at least during my high school years, that Christianity does indeed "make a difference."

When I attended college I majored in the social sciences. In the course of study, I became aware that the education people receive, the income they earn, their work environments and a host of other factors affect their outlook and behavior. It became obvious that many forces, in addition to religion, have an impact on people's lives and, insofar as this book is concerned, their marriages and family life.

I was also struck by how members of various social classes and cultures often subscribe to highly divergent convictions about reality, and by the seeming inconsistencies in their claims. Yet I was impressed by the potential of social science research methodology to assess the validity of many of these claims. By devising scientific (empirically testable) hypotheses and obtaining appropriate data, many of these claims could be objectively verified or nullified.

I fully realize that these methods are not appropriate for determining the reality of God or of certain beliefs about Him. I also acknowledge that some people will take exception to these methods and those who would apply them because they feel threatened or misunderstood. Yet I stand convinced that social science methods, when combined with other means of examination and discovery, can be immensely valuable in the pursuit of truth. These methods are useful tools for assessing many of the claims that people make about marriage and the family and about the alleged impact that religion (and other forces) has on the marriage and family relationship. Moreover, carefully conceived and conducted research can provide insight into areas in which people and their marriages are hurting, as well as the causes of this hurt. These insights can be helpful in devising productive ways to respond to these problem areas. It is my hope that the material presented in this book will heighten perception of the pressures and problems confronting couples in contemporary suburban marriages and provide direction to those concerned with productively responding to them.

I wish to extend the following grateful acknowledgments: to Bee-Lan Wang for her helpful suggestions during the early phases of the study design; to Pauline Roelofs for her help in preparing the initial and final drafts of the questionnaire and interview schedule; to the many couples we interviewed who gave so liberally of their time while sharing many intimate details of their marriages; to those who conducted the interviews and to those who helped in coding the information; to Wheaton College and to Northwest Nazarene College for providing grants to assist in data collection and analysis; to Kevin Dennis who acted as one of my harshest critics as he assessed the literary quality of the manuscript; to Lorna Nganga for the many insights she offered in interpreting data obtained from the respondents; to Bob and Donna Oehrig for their helpful comments on early drafts of the manuscript; to Jennifer Lincoln Hansen for her assistance in pulling together the last chapter of the manuscript; to my editor, Terry Trepper, who painstakingly reviewed my initial manuscript and offered numerous and insightful suggestions for revision; to my daughter, Kelley, who endured episodes of my paying more attention to the data analysis and manuscript preparation than to her.

Chapter 1

Christiantown Families:
The Yuppy Generation

This book is based on a study of family life in a community which we have chosen to call Christiantown because it is viewed by many as a center of religious organizational activity. Unlike so much of what one reads or hears these days, it is not based on hearsay or speculation. On the contrary, it is based on the lives and experiences of fifty couples who participated in a study of marital and parental adjustment, communication, and conflict resolution, and who reported about themselves. The study addresses the impact of religion on marriage relationships, and focuses on how these relationships are affected by work and money and sex. It examines how the current generation of couples are adapting to increased occupational status, new and more egalitarian patterns of decision-making, and smaller family size. Also noted are the coping strategies couples use to adjust to marital conflict and the demands of child rearing; as well as the everyday life concerns and problems of people residing in suburbia.

The findings reported in this study should provide valuable insight and direction to pastors, counselors, social workers, program planners, and other professionals seeking to respond meaningfully to the needs of married parents and their families. The findings should also be of interest to laymen seeking a general knowledge of the contemporary family and to social scientists interested in assessing the impact of numerous forces on the family.

MOTIVATION FOR INVESTIGATION

From its inception, a predominant concern of this study has been to assess the nature of religion's impact on marriage and family life. There are two major reasons why such assessment is important. First, it helps to expose inappropriate, misleading, and sometimes debilitating stereotypes for what they are. Second, it helps to clarify the nature and extent of problems in need of attention.

Until recently there has been little scientific study of the nature of religion's impact on marriage and family relationships. What studies were available tended to treat religion rather casually, reporting to have measured it by means of a question or two concerning religious affiliation or church attendance.

CONTRASTING IMPRESSIONS

In the absence of available and reliable data on the state of the Christian family, pronouncements have tended toward extremes. On the one hand there are those who maintain that Christian marriages are not only different from, but far superior to, all other (non-Christian) marriages. Their view maintains that the Christian family is healthier, happier, better adjusted, and more prosperous—in short, it has more of the good things that one might look for in a marriage. On the other hand, there are those who insist that such assertions are merely a sales pitch. They see Christians as people afflicted with the same shortcomings as their non-Christian neighbors, and believe any semblance of superior well-being among Christian couples and families is superficial at best. Some critics even assert that Christian couples and their families are worse off because of theological rigidity (Hadden, 1983; Larsen, 1978; Scanzoni, 1983). Alleged conflicts include the aggressive exercise of "divine" authority by husbands over their wives and by parents over their children. They also include the supposed reluctance of some Christians to admit their sexual nature, a problem that results in sexual suppression with its associated problems of poor sexual communication and lack of fulfillment.

How are these contrasting claims to be explained? Advocates of each position maintain that their perspectives are valid, and by inference, each maintains that the claims of the other are false. After listening to proponents of the respective positions, it seems that much of the polarity on this issue is due more to presupposition than to fact (McNamara, 1985a). Some religionists are quite convinced, for example, that personal sin lies at the heart of every human problem, and that personal salvation from sin will solve all maladies. From this vantage point, the fact that Christian couples—those who, by God's divine grace, have been saved from sin—are in all respects better off than their non-Christian counterparts is a foregone conclusion.

Others operate from a different set of assumptions. Secular humanists, for example, are inclined to deny the potential of Christianity—or any religion—to significantly improve man's lot. In fact, some believe that religion interferes with and minimizes the humanizing and mutually self-actualizing potential of marital relationships—a value which the humanists tend to prize. The suggestion that Christian couples are in any way better off than their non-Christian counterparts is, for them, preposterous. On the contrary, they would argue that because of trappings like dogmatism and self-righteousness, Christian couples are actually worse off. For them, this "truth" is a foregone conclusion (McNamara, 1985b).

Those of us who have attempted to base our assessment on something more than ideological bias and attention-getting media imagery have often had little more to go on than the impressions of pastors, counselors, attorneys, and psychologists, whose experiences are generally limited to a small and rather atypical group of clients. Moreover, their studies have frequently attempted to assess the quality of Christian marriages more on inference than on explicit, in-depth measurement (Gruner, 1985, p. 48).

SOME PROVOCATIVE QUESTIONS

When preparing our interview materials, a number of questions came to mind. Just how and when does religion make a difference? What things tend to worry or concern spouses and parents the most?

Are the critics right in their suggestion that Christian couples have some serious problems?

To assess correctly the influence of religion on marriage, it is important to put it into appropriate perspective by considering the significance of other forces as well. What about the impact of education, job satisfaction, and income? What role do these forces play in establishing marital adjustment? How do they influence marital attraction?

Sociologists David and Vera Mace believe that the answer to this last question is of utmost significance in the context of contemporary society (Mace & Mace, 1974). They point out that the past few decades have witnessed the rapid withering of traditional constraints against divorce. In previous times the prospect of financial calamity kept many from seeking divorce. But in the context of today's relative affluence and the financial independence experienced by increasing numbers of working women, much of the financial risk has been removed. Another traditional constraint fast disappearing is the concern and consequence of tarnished reputation. Changing attitudes have substantially reduced this risk as well. As far as legal constraints are concerned, one thrice-divorced man summarized the situation when he mused that getting a divorce today is easier than taking a girl to the senior prom, and given the elaborateness of some proms, divorce can be less expensive as well.

Perhaps the behavior of churches, those traditional bastions of marital stability, portrays the changing situation best. With divorce becoming more prevalent among members, few churches are inclined to uphold divorce as a basis for removal from membership. Some have even eliminated divorce as a disqualification for church leadership. More and more one hears of special Sunday school classes and other church-sponsored programs for divorced persons. As if to give a measure of credibility to the institution of divorce, a few congregations have even devised public divorce ceremonies (*Chicago Tribune*, 1976).

Reflecting on the significance of these changes, the Maces conclude that marital stability today is less a matter of external coercion than it is a matter of internal cohesion (Mace & Mace, 1974). Yet this cohesion depends on people finding a sufficient measure of attraction in, and deriving a significant amount of satisfaction from, their marriages.

In our search for factors having a bearing on marital satisfaction and attraction, we were concerned about finding the answers to several related questions: (a) What role does religion play in making marriages attractive and satisfying? (b) How important is sexual satisfaction to marital happiness? (c) How does financial income affect marital satisfaction? (d) Are working wives inclined to be less satisfied with their marriages? (e) Is marital adjustment positively or adversely affected by the arrival of children? Questions such as these will be addressed in the upcoming chapters.

GENERATIONAL CHANGE

In addition to the changes that have had an impact on all members of our society, we found that Christiantowners departed from their parents in three significant respects. As a group, Christiantown couples have a higher occupational status, and therefore are likely to have a greater amount of education and income than their parents. They also manifest more egalitarian decision making where both husband and wife endeavor to make decisions jointly. Finally, they have chosen to have fewer children than their parents had. As we consider the well-being of Christiantown marriages, we will examine the impact of these factors.

WHY CHRISTIANTOWN?

The study site is Wheaton, Illinois. With its population of 43,000 (1980) and proximity to Chicago (approximately 25 miles) Wheaton accommodates a fair number of residents who commute the metropolis and those communities surrounding it. Although Wheaton residents manifest a fair array of religious beliefs and practices, because of the large number of church-related organizations located there (see Chapter 2 for details), we have referred to it as Christiantown.

The decision to select Christiantown as the locus of study was purposeful. For one thing, Christiantown demonstrates the suburbanization phenomenon which has so characterized American society during much of the 20th century. At the beginning of the century, less than one-fourth of the U.S. population lived in an area conveniently close to a city yet far enough away to be considered a suburb. In fact, the very concept of a suburb was scarcely recognized. By the 1950s, the suburbanization of the American family was well under way. Throughout the 1960s and into the 1970s, suburbs remained choice locations for couples seeking a climate they regarded as most suited to enjoying each other and raising a family. Compared to downtowns and city centers, suburbs were regarded as safer environments with better schools, churches, and medical and recreational facilities, all of which parents (and many other adults) look for in a community.

This brings us to a second reason for selecting Wheaton as a locus of study. In recent years crowded conditions, run-down housing, and escalating crime rates have caused many suburbs to lose much of their original luster. For example, Peters and Larkin (1983) note that more families still live in suburbia than reside in either central cities or rural areas, but many families with the necessary means have begun to move beyond suburb to country.

In the midst of these changes, some suburbs have successfully maintained their appeal to families, Christiantown is one such suburb. According to the 1980 census, the vast majority of dwellings in Christiantown are occupied by families. In fact, only 6.7% of family households were headed by a female with no spouse present (U.S. Bureau of the Census, 1988, p. 643). Although this figure is only slightly lower than several of the surrounding suburbs, it compares with other Chicago area suburbs such as Evanston (10.3%) and Park Forest Village (11.9%), and shows a marked contrast with "close-in" suburbs like Maywood Village (19.9%).

Whether so-called successful suburbs have actually managed to establish a climate conducive to building healthy and happy marriages and families is a matter of some debate. The quality of schools, churches, and community services is evident. But some fear that because these communities have served as a magnet for people who have moved up the ladder of status and financial success, the residents may place so much stress on personal and material achievement that marital health and family well-being are seriously jeopardized.

Are "successful suburb" residents finding satisfaction and fulfillment in their marriages? What worries and concerns occupy their minds? Is there evidence of a struggle for money and status and, if so, how does this affect marital satisfaction and parental adjustment? How well are successful suburb residents functioning as parents? These are some of the questions we hoped to answer in our study of Christiantowners.

THE TRADITION OF COMMUNITY STUDIES

The earliest attempt to systematically describe a community in America with scientific detachment was made by Robert and Helen Lynd back in 1925 and again in 1935 (Lynd & Lynd, 1929, 1937). A number of noteworthy community studies have been conducted since that pioneering work on "Middletown." These include such notable studies as Elmtown's Youth (Hollingshead, 1949); The Urban Villagers (Gans, 1962), The Levittowners (Gans, 1967), and Yankee City (Warner, 1963). These studies constitute important works in their own right, but it was the Lynds' study which so aptly demonstrated how qualitative and quantitative data could be blended together to yield a more complete picture of reality.

The methodological legacy that the Lynds left behind had an important impact on this research. Yet the Christiantown study was most consciously influenced by two other studies of marriage relationships. One was Blood and Wolfe's (1960) study *Husbands and Wives*. The authors sought there to understand the dynamics of marriage relationships by analyzing data secured from a number of highly structured interviews of married women residing in the Detroit area.

A second study which had a significant effect in shaping the Christiantown study was Mirra Komarovsky's (1962) *Blue-Collar Marriage*. In her effort to understand the marital experience of the blue-collar class, Komarovsky conducted case studies of 58 women and their husbands. She did so by posing a number of open-ended questions to respondents largely selected from a directory of a combined community of some 50,000 people located within five miles of a major metropolitan area which she called "Glenton."

Christiantown is a suburban community nearly the same size as Komarovsky's Glenton and not far (twenty-five miles) from a major metropolitan area. Like Komarovsky, our study incorporated extensive interviews with married spouses (fifty couples in all), and we used a number of open-ended questions. As in the Komarovsky study, husbands and wives were interviewed separately, and the principal investigator conducted a number of the interviews himself.

While the methodologies of our studies were similar in a number of respects, the populations we studied were quite different. Komarovsky reports that white-collar occupations constituted slightly more than a third of Glenton's labor force and that a little over a third of the residents had completed four years of high school. In contrast, the majority of Christiantown residents are white-collar professionals, with at least 58% of our sample falling in this occupational category. Moreover, 88% of the residents have at least 12 years of formal education and 40% of those over age 24 have completed college.

HOW WE CONDUCTED THE STUDY

Formal work on the Christiantown study began with a review of the literature. Literature review uncovered the latest findings, and also generated research questions in addition to those already proposed. I became intrigued, for example, with examining a possible connection between conservative religious beliefs and sexual behavior.

The literature also provided ideas about how to formulate survey and interview questions in order to explore the various areas of interest. In fact, whenever possible, I incorporated questions which had proven useful in other studies. (These included items used in both the Blood and Wolfe study and the Komarovsky study.) The inclusion of these items gave us some assurance that the questions would be clearly understood and would effectively elicit the kind of information we were seeking.

In selecting Christiantown residents for inclusion in the study, the following three concerns were paramount:

1. Participants must be selected on a truly random basis. It would have been easier to stand on the steps of one of Christiantown's many churches and to interview people as they came out the door following a Sunday morning service. Or, like some other studies, we could have published a questionnaire in a local publication and asked people to fill it out. Such methods generate sizable samples with minimum effort, but we felt it imperative that participants be selected at random from the population to insure that those included in the sample accurately represent the community under study.

2. Both husbands and wives had to be included. Several studies of marriage and family life have surveyed and interviewed wives but excluded husbands. This practice is understandable since wives are often more accessible than their husbands. Yet any effort to understand marital relationships and to compare husband and wife experiences and behaviors requires the inclusion of both husbands and wives in the study.

3. In order to determine the impact of children on marriage as well as the impact of factors such as religion on the parental experience, it was important to select a sample of parents.

To meet these criteria, the final sample was obtained from among those names appearing in three school directories. The procedure was to select every seventh name in numerical sequence. In this study, only families with both a father and mother living at home were included. Having selected the names, the next step was to send a letter announcing the nature of the study and then follow up with a phone call (or occasionally a personal visit) to arrange an appointment for an interview. Frequently, several contacts had to be made in order to arrange a suitable time when both the husband and wife could be present. When potential respondents had no phone, visits to the registered address were made.

Several college students were recruited to do the first phase of the interviewing. These students were given an orientation to interview technique, instructed on the need to read questions just as they appeared on the interview schedule, and advised of the importance of insuring and preserving confidentiality. To help insure that spouses would not influence one another in their responses, interviewers were also instructed to interview both spouses on the same occasion but with each spouse out of earshot of the other. The interviewers then conducted practice sessions. A meeting was held to discuss the results of these interview experiences, which provided an opportunity to answer questions and to solve potential problems. During this first phase fifty-two people were interviewed (twenty-six married couples), with approximately 68% of those contacted participating.

The second phase of the interviewing was more intensive than the first. In addition to the eighty-nine fixed-response questions used in the first phase, we introduced thirty-three additional open-ended questions. We predicted that the addition of these items would help provide valuable insight into the nature and quality of Christiantown marriages. This proved to be the case. The addition of these items required a revision in the interview procedure. While one spouse filled out the questionnaire, the thirty-one open-ended questions were orally presented to the other spouse. Following this session, the spouse interviewed first filled out the questionnaire while the other spouse was interviewed. Once again, each spouse was interviewed separately, to avoid influencing the other's responses. Both the questionnaire and the interview items appear in the appendix.

This procedure increased the time needed to complete the fieldwork. Consequently, our original goal called for including seventy-five couples in the sample, but this was revised downward to fifty couples (100 respondents). Just three interviewers were utilized in this second phase, with about a third of the interviews conducted by the principal investigator. In this second interviewing phase, our rate of participation approached 80%.[1]

Throughout the interviewing period, which covered the space of eight months in 1980, the interviewers and I generally enjoyed good rapport with our respondents, and most of the couples volunteered much more information than was formally requested. In fact, the moments following the interview—when the couple came back together—often proved to be a time of relaxed sharing and elaboration on topics addressed in the study. Interviewers, myself included, were often surprised by the amount of confidential information participants shared.

Despite efforts to avoid sample bias, some bias may have occurred. For example, a few couples could not be contacted or scheduled for an interview. If these tended to represent problem marriages, then these types of marriages were undersampled.

Our sample of study participants was unique in certain significant respects. We included only families in which both the father and mother were living together. People whose marriages had not lasted long enough to see at least one of their children into primary school were excluded. Also, given the predominantly white racial constituency of the community, our sampling procedure turned up only white respondents. Nor were many economically disadvantaged families included. Judging from reports of yearly income and financial worries, only a few were living at the lower end of the economic spectrum.

GUIDELINES FOR READING THIS BOOK

We noted earlier how people are often forced to rely on impressionistic hunches and media-conveyed images of marriage and family life because of a lack of scientific data. However, even when such data are available, they often appear in technical reports and scientific journals which are not generally accessible — much less easily understood — by the general public.

In writing this book, a special effort was made to avoid complex terminology and to present data in a readily understandable manner. Complex tables have been reduced to simple bar graphs. Most technical information has been relegated to footnotes and to the appendix. And lest the reader lose touch with the people behind the statistics, several references are made to specific people and the circumstances they face. Names and other identifying information have been changed to protect the privacy of the respondents, and details of some specific situations have been blended. Yet the case accounts remain accurate in revealing the nature and experience of Christiantown couples.

NOTE

1. Because the interviewing in phase one and phase two were done somewhat differently, we were curious to note whether these techniques were yielding different results. Upon comparing the composite marital adjustment scores and marital happiness levels of the two groups, we found the results to be very similar.

Chapter 2

Christiantown:
An All American City

Thank you Lord for the beautiful community you have given us to live in; for our families, for our jobs, and most of all, Lord, for our churches.

— Prayer offered at a Christiantown
businessman's prayer breakfast

Christiantown contains what most Americans look for in a suburb: lots of quiet, tree-lined streets; single-dwelling houses; quality schools; spacious and well-kept parks; a full range of churches; adjacent forest recreation land; and easy access to a major metropolis. Just as important, Christiantown lacks what many move to suburbia to avoid: polluted air, heavy industry, urban blight, hard-core poverty, and street crime. In many respects Christiantown would seem to be the perfect place to live. It is not surprising, then, that in nationwide competition in the late 1960s, this suburban town was named the "All American City."

A QUEST FOR CONTINUITY IN THE MIDST OF CHANGE

In the years since receiving this distinction, Christiantown appears to have undergone some change. Despite the efforts of some organizations to keep it quiet, one occasionally hears complaints of theft and even rape.

Some fear that crime is on the increase, but in fact only fourteen violent crimes were known by police to have occurred in all of 1985. This figure compares quite favorably to neighboring cities for which such statistics are available. For the same year Downer's Grove (population 42,400), reported fifty-three violent crimes, while Niles (population 29,480), reported thirty-seven violent crimes (U.S. Bureau of the Census, 1988, pp. 642, 643).

Although crime does not appear to have gotten a foothold in the community, high-rise housing shows signs of doing so. Concern over increased crowding has prompted some citizens to engage in a concerted grass roots effort to discourage further growth and development. In one instance this took the form of a "green-lining" campaign led by a local lawyer. The plan invoked pledges by various neighborhood groups to deposit money in banks in exchange for a bank agreement not to make loans to developers, and/or pledges to withdraw money from banks that did. In operation, the plan was supposed to have an effect similar to that of "red-lining."[1]

Some suburbs close to the central city have experienced increasing density and a measure of decay, but Christiantown has been able to keep its small-town atmosphere. In summer it is still common to see couples strolling through one of several well-maintained parks, kids feeding the ducks by the lake, and families taking in an outdoor concert courtesy of the municipal band. Saturday morning will find many kids taking their music lessons at the college, participating in one of several city recreational programs, or joining mom and dad for a swim at the local YMCA. All these activities occur in a climate of comparative safety and isolation from the kinds of problems that plague much of the outside world.

A CLIMATE OF PROSPERITY

The image of Christiantown residents conveyed in a local Chamber of Commerce publication is clearly upper-middle class:

> Many are executives of Chicago companies, and others are engineers or research scientists employed by the various industries in the immediate area. These people have similar educational backgrounds [and] salaries in the same general bracket. (Greater Wheaton Chamber of Commerce, 1985)

Our random sample of Christiantowners supports this imagery. Not only had all participants graduated from high school, but the majority (72%) held college degrees. In addition, a fair number (particularly men) had completed a course of post-college study at a professional school or university.

Consistent with their level of education, our sample of Christiantowners tend to have high-status occupations. On a seven-point occupational prestige index, well over half of the occupations of men in our sample measured within two points of the highest status level (Table 2.1).

In addition to education and occupation, a third means of assessing the prosperity of Christiantowners is income. On this measure Christiantowners again appear fairly well off. In fact, the average family income of Christiantowners places the city 28th on the list of some 200 Chicago-area suburbs (Greater Wheaton Chamber of Commerce, 1985). On a per capita basis, the average income of Christiantown residents is just over 139% of the average for the state (U.S. Bureau of the Census, 1988, p. 644). Less than 2% of Christiantown families fell below the poverty level for 1979.

Average education, income, and occupational status figures all attest to the authenticity of the Chamber of Commerce's claim that Christiantown residents, as a group, constitute a distinctive and prosperous citizenry. These averages, however, mask some of the diversity among Christiantown residents. While the nature of the city's retail businesses and "clean" industry comfortably accommodates people in the managerial and professional classes, some of Christiantown's primary breadwinners earn their living from low to mid-level sales and service occupations. Total income for these people places their families near the margin of economic survival. (See Appendix A, Table A.1 for an indication of income levels of study participants.)

A CONSERVATIVE BENT

According to one definition, a conservative is someone who has something to conserve and strives to conserve it. If that is true, Christiantown residents show definite signs of conservatism. This was evident in the "green-lining" campaign mentioned earlier. It

TABLE 2.1. Occupational Status Index

Status Level	Sample Occupations	Husbands	
Low		number	%
1	shoe shiner, servant garbage collector migrant worker	0	0
2	high school custodian industrial security worker railroad switchman factory worker	1	2
3	carpenter, construction worker, coal miner, coal miner, mail carrier	2	4
4	farmer, salesman, electrician maintenance supervisor	5	10
5	funeral director building contractor teacher, union officer automobile dealer newspaper reporter	12	24
6	commercial bank officer, college professor, pharmacist, minister, geologist	20	40
7	chemical engineer doctor, dentist, lawyer, patent attorney	9	18
High			
uncodeable		1	2
	total	50	100%

---

was also evident in one mayoral election in which the candidate who proposed to redevelop the downtown area by building an overnight lodge was soundly defeated. No such facility existed in Christiantown and, judging from the outcome of the election, residents were not about to change the status quo. The fact that the suburban county, of which Christiantown is the county seat, has routinely resisted applying for federal low-income housing funds also fits the prevailing pattern.

The town's conservatism is also evident in state and national politics. In terms of organization, support, and visibility, the conservative Republican party wins hands down over the rival Democrats. In primary elections, Republican candidates routinely outnumber Democrats, and in run-off elections Republican party candidates typically take the majority of votes. It comes as no surprise that in recent presidential elections, residents have voted for Republican presidential candidates by wide margins.

A RELIGIOUS CENTER – WITH A SECULAR SIDE

A former missionary to Africa relates this story about a young Nigerian boy whose lifelong dream was to visit Christiantown. As the story goes, this lad had learned to read and write in a mission school and found himself surrounded with Christian literature. It seemed that every time he picked up a Bible, a periodical, or a book it would say, "Published in Christiantown, U.S.A." When at last his lifelong wish came true and the New York skyline came into view from the air, his comment was, "If this huge city is New York, I can't wait to see Christiantown."

This story makes its point well. For a city with less than 50,000 residents, Christiantown's phone directory reads like a who's-who of Christian organizations. Not only are publishers such as Scripture Press and Tyndale House located here, but the city is also home for organizations such as the National Association of Evangelicals, Bibles for the World, Youth For Christ, the Conservative Baptist Association of America, the National Association of Christian Schools, Missionary Services, Gideons International, World Relief Commission, and the Lausanne Committee for World Evangelism, to mention but a few. Cognizant of this heavy gathering of conservative Christian organizations, the news media have dubbed Christiantown "The Evangelical Vatican."

Historically Christiantown and Christianity have been closely aligned. The course was set over a century ago when Wheaton College, a major nondenominational evangelical school, was founded in Christiantown within a year of the city's charter. Partially due to the early presence of the college, the city presently boasts the heaviest concentration of evangelical organizations in the world.

These observations may imply that Christiantown constitutes a sort of Protestant monoculture, yet there is evidence of a fair amount of religious diversity. Although our random sample of Christiantowners turned up a majority of Protestants, a significant 18% identified themselves as Catholic. In addition to two churches, Catholics have a well-established grade school and high school. The 90-acre nursing-care center operated by the Franciscan Sisters further testifies to the non-Protestant presence.

Other facilities reveal a religious representation beyond Christendom. The international Theosophical Society has long maintained its headquarters in Christiantown. In addition to its administrative offices, the society runs a sizable book shop conspicuously located on one of the choicest pieces of real estate in town.

The prominence of the religious presence in Christiantown has not ruled out a secular presence as well. The institution which is perhaps most responsible for the town's reputation is Wheaton College. Yet this institution is easily dwarfed by the nearby junior college which, in terms of full-time and part-time enrollment, is almost ten times larger.[2] Moreover, the atmosphere on this junior college campus is avidly secular, with students expressing and acting out values in sharp contrast to those espoused by much of the Christian community. This became apparent to us just prior to the study. Students at Wheaton studied heterosexual behavior among students on the two campuses, using questionnaires that were filled out anonymously. They found only a small percentage of the Wheaton students sampled indicated that they had ever had premarital sex. This was in striking contrast to the trend which emerged from the secular campus classroom sample in which sexual abstainers were in the distinct minority.

These observations should give one a general "feel" for the climate of Christiantown. To many observers, Christiantown presents an enviable exterior. But what about its interior? Are Christiantown marriages as neat and well ordered as the community? In the following chapters we will describe this interior in some detail. We shall begin by examining the marital health and well-being of the residents.

NOTES

1. After early efforts to get this campaign started, it fizzled and died; a prominent Christiantown banker cannot recall any pressure having been put on his bank to limit loans to developers.

2. The College of DuPage is a public junior college with over 20,000 full- and part-time students. It is located in the adjacent town of Glen Ellyn.

Chapter 3

The Quality
of Christiantown Marriages

*In [Christiantown], the All-American city, they try to show the
general public one thing but actually live under another. . . .
On the outside, they [Christiantowners] are righteous, pious,
successful . . . but on the inside they're literally falling apart.*

— Rev. Thomas Nielsen (Wexler, 1980)

How healthy are Christiantown marriages? Are they as successful
as some of their prosperous exteriors suggest? Or do they resemble
the whitewashed tombs with which Christ compared the Scribes and
Pharisees in the book of Matthew: beautiful on the outside but full
of rot and decay within?

In this chapter we shall examine the state of Christiantown marriages. Before beginning our analysis, though, a brief introduction
to the married couples who participated in our study is in order.

As noted in the introductory chapter, we selected our respondents
from school directories on a random basis. Consequently, those included in our sample had several years of marriage experience.
Most of the couples we interviewed had been married between nine
and nineteen years; their ages ranged between twenty-seven and
fifty-two though the majority were in their thirties. In accordance
with the national trend, the wives we sampled tended to marry at a
somewhat younger age than their husbands. While the age at which
the couples married ranged between a low of seventeen and a high
of thirty-five, the average age (just above twenty-four years) indicates that our respondents married at a somewhat older age than
most U.S. couples (Dolmatch, 1980). Since most of our respon-

dents (72%) were college graduates, we suspect that this in part reflects the tendency of a number of our respondents to delay marriage until they completed college.

Selecting study participants from school directories also helped insure that all of them would have experience as parents. Actual family size (husband and wife plus natural and/or adopted children) ranged between three and eight. Most families had two or three children.

THE QUALITY OF CHRISTIANTOWN MARRIAGES

To assess the health and well-being of Christiantown marriages, we incorporated a number of specific questions concerning the way couples relate to each other, their contentment with their marriage, and with each other, etc. Lest our appraisal of Christiantown marriages reflect only our criteria of well-being, we also posed some very general questions. For example, we asked several respondents to comment on what they considered to be the most satisfactory aspect of their marriage, what they would like to see changed, and what they saw as the key to marital success. Open-ended questions have the advantage of allowing respondents to give responses as long and as varied as they desire. The responses bearing on marital well-being centered around three areas: marital happiness, marital communication and companionship, and overall marital adjustment.

HOW HAPPY ARE THEY?

Of the three areas, surveying marital happiness is probably the most common means of assessing the quality of American marriages. The commitment to pursuing happiness runs deep in our cultural tradition, and most people view marriage as worthwhile to the degree that the arrangement leads to personal happiness.

Our determination of the marital happiness of Christiantowners was straightforward. We asked each of our respondents to indicate the spot on a number line which best describes the degree of happiness of their marriage (Figure 3.1).[1]

The distribution of happiness ratings generated by this question is

FIGURE 3.1. Marital Happiness Rating Scale

```
==================================================================

     0     5     10    15    20    25    30

     ._____._____._____._____._____._____.

   Very                  Happy                  Perfectly
 Unhappy                                          Happy

------------------------------------------------------------------
```

noteworthy. Only 5% of our respondents indicated that they were unhappily married by rating their marriage at ten or below on the scale. On the other hand, fully 87% rated their marriage at twenty or above. Moreover, 65% placed their marriage at the top end of the scale (between twenty-five and thirty). Henceforth we will refer to this latter group of marriages as "very happy."

These findings are interesting in themselves, but it is helpful to compare these results with other studies. Three national studies conducted in the mid to late 1970s found that 68% of married adults surveyed rated their marriages as "very happy" (Leslie, 1982). Our percentage of "very happy" marriages (65%) comes surprisingly close to the national average.

The updated study of Middletown, better known as Muncie, Indiana provides another useful comparison (see Caplow et al., 1982). This study found that the percentage of "very happy" marriages hovered around 50% for the working class and rose to a high of 60% for the business class. In terms of this comparison, it seems that Christiantowners, who reside in a more suburban area, appear to fare quite well.

WHO ARE MORE HAPPILY MARRIED: MEN OR WOMEN?

A number of studies have found that men tend to be more happily married than women. For example, in the Muncie, Indiana study just referred to, it was found that the extent of "very happy" marriages among men was between seven and ten percentage points higher than those for women. In her book, *The Future of Marriage*, Jessie Bernard comments on this difference and concludes that being married is a much better deal for men than it is for women (Bernard, 1972). Whether it is measured in terms of mental health, freedom from criminal activity, career success, or sheer survival, research reveals that married men fare significantly better than their never-married counterparts. Yet many of these gains either do not accrue or are much less apparent with married women. Both Bernard and Gove (1972) argue that for women, marital roles tend to be stressful and confining and limit their opportunities.

On the basis of Bernard's observations, we might well expect the marital happiness ratings for Christiantown women to be substantially below those for men. On a scale from zero (very unhappy) to thirty (perfectly happy) the average happiness rating for women (22.4) does fall somewhat below the average for men (23.7), but in view of the larger trend, this difference is surprisingly slight. Since these figures are averages, it is possible that they mask some differences. It may be worth noting that of the five people who rated their marriages as unhappy, four of them were women.

Happiness ratings are certainly not the only basis for determining whether women tend to get short shrift in the marriage "deal." Consequently we shall examine possible differences in the marriage experience of husbands and wives in upcoming chapters. (This issue is dealt with most directly in the discussion of sex roles in Chapter 11.)

TWO SIGNIFICANT DIMENSIONS: COMMUNICATION AND COMPANIONSHIP

A criticism directed at studies which use marital happiness ratings as their major basis for determining marital satisfaction is that their measure gives no indication of what makes people happy. To get an idea of people's thoughts in this regard, we asked approximately half of our respondents what they considered to be the most satisfactory aspect of their marriage. Although the terminology varied, respondents referred more often to some aspect of companionship than to anything else. One wife who had been married nine years said that she found the most satisfaction in "doing all things together like sailing, camping—even household chores." Another woman in a thirteen-year marriage said that "doing things together that are physically healthy, enjoying sporting activities and being out in the natural environment" was her greatest source of marital satisfaction.

Companionship may be the most frequently mentioned source of marital satisfaction, but communication comes in a close second. Commenting on what they found most satisfying about their marriage, some Christiantowners simply mentioned "communication." Others elaborated on the concept by expressing satisfaction with a partner with whom they could share their innermost thoughts. Of course companionship and communication are closely related, and we were not surprised to find some respondents mentioning these two sources of satisfaction almost in the same breath.

In addition to asking our respondents to comment on sources of marital satisfaction, we also asked them what, if anything, they would like to see changed in their marriage. Nearly half of those responding mentioned the lack of sufficient time together. Others, after commenting on a variety of specifics, expressed a desire for more companionship. Christiantowners not only prize the companionship they have found in marriage, but they often long for still more of it.

Studies indicate that Christiantowners are not unlike other contemporary couples in the stress they place on companionship. Several sociologists have indicated that this emphasis is much greater today than it was in the past, although they tend to disagree on the reasons for this change. Ernest Burgess and his associates believe that because past generations have, for the most part, been primarily concerned about sheer economic survival, they could not afford to be preoccupied with companionship (Burgess et al., 1971). Moreover, the formal authority structure and division of labor which emerged to help insure such survival supposedly did little to encourage person-based companionship.

Other sociologists such as William Goode (1970) see the current emphasis on companionship as a response to a highly specialized society. In a time of relatively low occupational specialization, chances are that most people knew Betty Forbes not simply as the town librarian but as Ben Forbes' wife, Paul and Steve's mother, and the pianist at the First Presbyterian Church. Today people must necessarily interact with a number of people in a wide range of occupations. This mitigates against getting to know each one of these people as persons in their own right. Thus when asked about Mrs. Jones, the librarian, a typical response might well be, "Oh, I get waited on by so many people at the library that I really don't know which one you mean."

According to Goode, people in all societies need to be accepted, understood, and appreciated as persons. He observes that within the context of today's highly specialized society, the family functions as a kind of psychic service station, enabling its members to cope with a rather cold and impersonal world. From William Goode's perspective, companionship marriage has become a practical necessity.

Whether or not our highly specialized world is as cold and impersonal as some claim it is, one fact remains. As a consequence of occupational specialization, people often find it necessary to move to where their specialized skills are in demand. The college student who majors in chemistry or psychology can plan on having to move to where he/she can get a job. This may well mean relocating to another state, away from relatives and friends. When married people make such moves they may well find that their companionship marriage helps sustain them in the process.

ASSESSING COMMUNICATION AND COMPANIONSHIP

From the responses of our study participants, it is clear that companionship can take on many forms in marriage. A couple may, for example, enjoy intellectual companionship in which they share thoughts and ideas as they might when preparing to vote in an upcoming political election. Or they may experience work companionship as they take on a common project such as remodeling their home.

To help assess the actual level of companionship and communication existing between Christiantown couples, we inquired about the extent to which couples engage in certain activities together. We asked our respondents to indicate how often they (a) laugh together, (b) calmly discuss something together, (c) have a stimulating exchange of ideas, and (d) work together on a project.[2]

The frequency with which people engage in these activities is summarized in Figure 3.2. We found that the first two items, calm discussion and mutual laughter, occur fairly frequently. It is apparent that our couples are not only on talking terms, but they *take time to talk*. The fact that they also laugh together fairly often suggests that they find their encounters enjoyable.

The last two items, exchanging ideas and working together on a project, occur less often. This may seem to imply that these couples, while engaging in discussion and laughing together fairly frequently, fail to communicate or interact at a deeper level. Yet fully 85% of our respondents indicated that they have a "stimulating exchange of ideas" at least once a week, and about the same percentage report working on a joint project at least once a month. The difference in the frequency with which people report engaging in

FIGURE 3.2. Frequency with which people engaged in four activities with their spouse

```
===============================================================

Activity                        Percent of People
 (number)                         Participating
----------------------------------------------------------------


Calm
Discussion      ******************82%***********************

Laugh
Together        ******************81%*********************.

Exchange of
Ideas           *******30%*****

Work Together
on a Project    ***18%***

```

the four activities probably reflects the greater time and effort that some of these activities require.

Our four indicators do not exhaust all possible dimensions of companionship. They do suggest, however, that Christiantown couples are involved in what we term "companionship marriages." Yet, as we have observed, many husbands and wives would like to have still more companionship.

If companionship is what people are most happy about, then marital happiness should increase as companionship increases. We checked this out by combining the scores on the four companionship items into a composite index. Figure 3.3 compares our respondents' standing on this index with their happiness ratings. The relationship apparent in this figure is consistent with a growing volume of studies which indicate that the more time couples spend talking and in other ways engaging in joint activities, the greater their marital satisfaction (Miller, 1976; Orthner, 1975; Fowers & Olson, 1986).

MEASURING MARITAL ADJUSTMENT

Another frequently used barometer of marital well-being is adjustment. Simply stated, adjustment concerns how well spouses accommodate to one another. One means of measuring marital adjustment is the Locke-Wallace Short Marital Adjustment Test (Locke & Wallace, 1959). In assessing marital adjustment, the instrument incorporates such items as contentment with marriage and with the spouse (including marital happiness), common interests and activity, and consensus concerning major issues in marriage. This index has proven useful in a variety of studies (Barling, 1984; Holloway, 1987; Sporakowski & Hughston, 1978). We also found the index helpful in assessing the marital well-being of Christiantowners.[3]

The marital adjustment scores for our sample of Christiantowners ranged from a low of just 55 to a high of 153. The authors of the Locke-Wallace index suggest that the average high adjustment score is 136 and that the average low adjustment score is 72. Using these figures as reference points, the distribution of Christiantowner

FIGURE 3.3. Percentage of Very Happily Married according to level of companionship

===

Companionship Level	Percent Very Happily Married
(number)	

Low   ******************. 39%
(n=23)

Medium   *********************·***************. 69%
(n=42)

High   *** 80%
(n=35)

Spearman Rank Order Correlation = .40; p ≤ .001

scores looks quite favorable. Fully 87% of Christiantown marriages fall in the "good" to "very good" categories of adjustment.

Keeping in mind the continuing debate over how well women fare in marriage relative to men, we computed the averages separately for the two sexes. As in the case of marital happiness, the average adjustment score for women (120.9) is slightly below that for men (121.5). Given the broad range of scores for both men and women, the fact that the averages should be so close is surprising. In fact the small difference between them is so slight that there is no statistical significance. On the basis of marital happiness and adjustment, there is no clear indication that Christiantown husbands fare any better than their wives.[4]

Thus far we have assessed the quality of Christiantown marriages in terms of happiness levels, communication and companionship, and overall marital adjustment. In terms of these criteria, the average Christiantown marriage appears to be functioning well. However, these measures also indicate a fair amount of variation, with some spouses scoring relatively high and others scoring low. In the next chapter we will examine how religion affects these indicators of marital well-being.

NOTES

1. This technique has been used for many years by other investigators. Harvey J. Locke and Karl M. Wallace, "Short Marital-Adjustment and Prediction Tests: Their Reliability and Validity", *Marriage and Family Living*, (August, 1959), pp. 251-255.

2. Index taken from Boyd C. Collins and Herald Feldman, *Journal of Marriage and the Family* (February 1970), pp. 20-28.

3. While this index is much shorter than the Dyadic Adjustment Scale (Spanier, 1976), O'Leary & Turgewitz (1978) report that the index retains its validity and reliability.

4. This finding is substantiated by that of Holloway (1987) who used a similar age-group. This study used the Locke-Wallace index to help assess stress levels of two-generation farm families. The study revealed a mere two-point difference between the average scores of 104.5 and 102.5 for married sons and daughters respectively.

Chapter 4

Religion and Married Life

*What is the key to marital success? To seek God continually.
To understand and apply God's purpose for marriage.*

—41-year-old father of two.
Occupation: engineer's assistant.

After a two and one-half year courtship, much of which took place on a Christian college campus, Mat and Emily Bradley were convinced that they were right for each other and took the step into matrimony. Although more detached observers may have pointed out that their backgrounds were quite different (Mat came from a rural background and Emily from an urban middle-class background), the two of them were convinced that their love for each other, their love for God, and their commitment to a life of dedicated ministry to others would bind them together. From this standpoint, they certainly seemed to have a lot in common. Moreover, their Christian upbringing had instilled in them a strong religious faith and a firm conviction that God would see them through any difficulty they might encounter.

After graduating from college, Mat and Emily both secured teaching jobs in a private Christian grade school. The pay was not very much and the work was time-consuming, but buoyed by their idealism, the couple threw themselves into their "ministry." In their second year of teaching, Emily got pregnant. Although she initially considered continuing with her teaching career, Mat disapproved. Emily dutifully complied with her husband's wishes and quit her job.

Their son, Mark, was born during the next academic term, an

event they heralded with great pleasure. Yet with Mark's birth, differences in their respective backgrounds began to manifest. Mat, who grew up on a farm, was firm in his conviction that child rearing and child care were women's work. Yet Emily confided how much she had longed to see her husband become more involved in the care of their son. There was another problem: making and holding onto friendships. As new parents, Mat and Emily found that they had little in common with old friends who were still single or with those who had gotten married but had no children. Both had hoped that they would be able to make new friends at their church, yet what the two of them looked for in their friends was so different that they could not make friends in common.

Nearly nine years have elapsed since Mark was born and the Bradley's now have a second son. Yet time for this couple has been a poor healer and the problems they encountered so many years ago are still very much with them. Though they are actively involved with their church, they still have few friends in common.

When asked what he would most like to see changed in their relationship, Mat said he wishes that his wife had more self-confidence. Yet in a separate conversation, Emily told us how she had found much fulfillment in her teaching ministry and that in giving it up, a little of her self seemed to die. In her own mind, Emily clearly sees this as a spiritual problem, even suggesting that if she just had a more Christian attitude, she would not feel this way. As a Christian wife, Emily is convinced that her duty lies in obeying her husband. But when Emily was asked what *she* would like to see changed, she said, "Mat's personality. You just can't confront him. Our oldest son is finding this very difficult to deal with."

THE IMPACT OF RELIGION ON MARRIAGE

Religion seems to have had an impact on the Bradleys' marriage. But studies seeking to determine religion's impact on marriage relationships and family life have come up with various and often inconsistent results. In one recent study entitled *American Couples*, Philip Blumstein and Pepper Schwartz report on their study of 12,000 people across the United States. Analyzing their results, these investigators state: "Only a few of our findings indicate that relationships can be affected by attendance at church or synagogue" (Blumstein & Schwartz, 1983, p. 24). Yet contrasting these findings are those of Theodore Caplow and his associates (1982). Based on their study of Muncie, Indiana ("Middletown") residents, these investigators found church attendance to be related to both marital happiness and marital stability.

Although studies such as these are inconclusive concerning religion's impact on marriage, a number of our religiously conservative respondents were quite certain that religion is the key ingredient to marital success, and that the very foundation for happy and productive marriage relationships rests on a proper relation and respect for God. Are these people's convictions supported by the evidence?

In the course of our study we found that there are some commonly examined dimensions of religion which do not appear to have much impact on marriage. We also discovered that there are some often overlooked aspects of religion that have a considerable impact on marital relationships. In this chapter we will explore possible reasons for the varying results.

WHAT DOES IT MEAN TO BE RELIGIOUS?

Those who stress the importance of religion for family life generally state or imply that the more religious one is, the greater religion's impact. Yet here a problem emerges. What does it mean to be religious? And how do we determine the extent or degree of religious devotion? The ways people answer this question likely reflect the particular religious tradition from which they come. For example, someone steeped in Buddhist tradition would describe a "religious" person quite differently from someone reared in the Muslim or Jewish faith. The task of assessing religion—what social scientists refer to as "religiosity"—is a most difficult one.

The fact that the majority of our respondents either identify with the Christian tradition or use it as a frame of reference eased our task somewhat. In studying the impact of religion on marriage, we shall, therefore, focus attention on Christianity and assess religiosity in terms of certain experiences, beliefs, and behaviors that are regarded as important to a significant segment of the evangelical Christian community.

THE EXPERIENTIAL DIMENSION OF RELIGION

A common means by which Christians themselves assess whether or not a person is a "genuine" Christian is to determine whether that person has sought God's forgiveness for his/her sins and is endeavoring to live a life in accordance with God's will. In terms of these markers, our respondents rate quite high. Fully 85% of them answered affirmatively to the statement: "I have asked God's forgiveness for my sins and I know He forgives me." Furthermore, the vast majority of those agreeing with this statement also report that they try to live according to their concept of God's will for them.

Do those who have "sought" and "found" forgiveness from sin enjoy happier and healthier marriages than those who do not? Do those who are committed to living their lives according to God's will experience higher levels of marital satisfaction than those who do not? There is some evidence to suggest that they may (Gruner, 1985), yet our comparison of these groups fails to reveal any noteworthy difference. If we were to assess religion's impact in terms of these measures alone, the assertion that religion "makes all the difference" would not be accurate, at least for the majority of people in our study.

THE BELIEF DIMENSION OF RELIGION

The Christian community places great stress on "proper" religious beliefs. After all, one's very salvation, so some would maintain, may well depend on holding certain beliefs or faith convictions. And since "right" behavior is understood to flow from "right" belief, it was appropriate for us to give it due consideration.

In investigating religious belief, we incorporated four sets of belief statements used in previous studies (Stellway, 1973, 1976) which reflect beliefs about the nature of God, Jesus, Heaven, and the Bible (see Appendix A). Following the lead of other investigators (Stark & Glock, 1970), we constructed a composite index of doctrinal conservatism by assigning one point for each conservative belief statement a respondent endorsed, and then adding these together. Having determined where people fell on our conservative belief index, we were in a position to determine what, if any, correspondence exists between this and our indicators of marital well-being.

HOW ARE RELIGIOUS BELIEF AND MARITAL STABILITY RELATED?

It has been charged that contemporary Americans take commitment to job and career much more seriously than commitment to marriage. If this is true, it would seem not to apply to conservative Christians who view marriage as a sacred institution, the bonds of which should not be broken except by death. Conservative Christian leaders have tended to outspokenly criticize divorce and those who seek to dissolve their marriage by such means. In an effort to determine the impact of religious belief on divorce, we asked our respondents whether they had ever considered divorcing their spouse. As can be seen from Figure 4.1 highly conservative believers are somewhat more inclined to report that they have never considered divorcing their spouse.

This finding may be of considerable interest to some, but it reveals comparatively little about the actual quality of the husband-wife relationship. Marital happiness and adjustment do a better job of assessing quality. But do people with conservative beliefs enjoy greater marital happiness and adjustment than those with less conservative beliefs? One study did find some evidence of this (Hunt & King, 1978), but since marital adjustment in that study was inferred (Gruner, 1985), the results are somewhat tentative. Our analysis revealed no connection between religious belief and either marital happiness or adjustment.[1] Thus on the basis of our study, we cannot conclude that religious beliefs per se favorably affect the quality of marriage.

DOES RELIGIOUS BELIEF AFFECT THE MARRIAGE RELATIONSHIP?

An issue which has grown in proportion to the rise of the feminist movement concerns biblical teaching about the role of women in the marriage relationship. A number of conservative Christian writ-

FIGURE 4.1. Respondents indicating that they had never considered divorcing their spouse by level of religious conservatism

==

Religious Conservatism Index Score (number)	Percent Having Never Considered Divorce

- -

Highly Conservative
(scale score of 4)
(N=31)   ** 84%

Moderately Conservative
(scale score of 2-3)
(N=42)   ********************************** 62%

Less Conservative
(scale score of 0-1)
(N=25)   ************************************** 72%

- -

Spearman Rank Order Correlation (with uncollapsed categories) = (−).36; p = ≤.001

ers maintain that Scripture clearly teaches that wives must be submissive to their husbands (Christenson, 1970; LaHaye & LaHaye,
1976). Given the pervasiveness of this teaching in conservative
Christian circles (McNamara, 1985b), we suspected that conservative believers would also maintain that the Bible supports wifely
obedience to her husband. Figure 4.2 shows this to be the case;
depending on their level of conservatism, people differ in their support of this conviction by wide margins. In fact, virtually all of the
most conservative believers support the idea that the Bible teaches
wifely obedience to the husband.[2]

Having noted the tendency for the most conservative believers to
affirm the Bible's teaching concerning wifely submission, we suspected that they would relate to their spouses differently than less
conservative believers. Other writers (Hadden, 1983; Scanzoni,
1983) have suggested that this group of believers manifests the husband-dominant and wife-subservient pattern of relating to which the
Bradleys (the couple featured at the beginning of this chapter) so
closely conform. To test this hypothesis, we asked each of our respondents to think of an issue over which they and their spouse
most disagree and then to indicate what generally happens when
disagreements arise concerning this issue. Does the wife generally
give in? Does the husband? Or is the issue more often resolved by
mutual give-and-take?[3]

If our hypothesis was correct, we should have found that more
conservative believers say that the wife gives in. This, we thought,
would be most in keeping with what they believe the Bible teaches.
We were therefore surprised to find that highly conservative believers were no more inclined to resolve marital disagreements by the
wife's giving in to her husband's wishes than were those holding
less conservative beliefs. Regardless of their religious beliefs, the
majority of our respondents indicated that they resolved their most
frequent disagreement by mutual give and take (Figure 4.3).

These results concern the area of most frequent disagreement.
But what about marital disagreements in general? Perhaps our hypothesis would hold true in such instances. To examine this possibility we asked each of our marriage partners whether in general,
when disagreements arise, they usually result in the husband's giving in, the wife's giving in, or agreement by mutual give-and-take.

FIGURE 4.2. Responses to the statement: "A Christian wife should obey her husband"

```
==================================================================

Conservatism Level              Percent Agreeing with Statement
    (number)                                  [**]
------------------------------------------------------------------

Highly Conservative
(scale score of 4)
    (N=30)     ***************************97%*****************************.


Moderately Conservative
(scale score between 2 and 3)
    (N=26)     *******************58%*****************
Less Conservative
(scale score of 0 or 1)
    (N=25)     *****************56%**************
------------------------------------------------------------------

Kruskal-Wallis H = 14.55; p = ≤.001
```

FIGURE 4.3. Respondents' Religious Conservatism and their means for resolving great disagreements

```
==============================================================

Religious                Means of Conflict Resolution
Conservatism
(number)                            Percent
--------------------------------------------------------------

                         Husband    Wife       Mutual
                         Gives In   Gives in   Give and Take
--------------------------------------------------------------

Highly Conservative      xx17.9%xx ==17.9%== ****** 64.1% *******

(scale score of
3 to 4, n = 40)

Less Conservative        xxx20%xxxx ==15%==. ******* 65% ********

(scale score of
0 to 2, n = 39)

[xx] Husband Gives In
[==] Wife Gives In
[**] Agreement by Mutual Give and Take
--------------------------------------------------------------
```

38

As it turned out, 85% of our respondents indicated that they typically resolve all marital disagreements by give-and-take. Once again there was no indication that doctrinally conservative believers were any more inclined to depart from the give-and-take means of resolving conflict than were others.

We proceeded to look for other evidence of husband dominance in areas of sex and money management. In these areas as well, we failed to find a significant difference between highly conservative believers and those with less conservative beliefs. Based on our data, we find no support for the popular stereotype which portrays highly conservative Christian husbands as authoritarian male chauvinists. Nor do we find support for the complementary stereotype that doctrinally conservative wives are inclined to be docile and easily exploited by their husbands. These images, if they have ever been valid, simply do not appear to apply to the residents of Christiantown. We are even inclined to question the extent to which they apply to others outside of Christiantown. McNamara (1985b) observes that writers such as Hadden (1983) and Hunter (1983), who have pointed to the dangerous marital consequences which accrue a commitment to a belief in the authority of the husband and in the duty of wife's obedience, have failed to note whether these views are linked to actual behavior. Our research suggests the danger of assuming such a link.

RELIGIOUS BELIEF AND FAMILY SIZE

One area where religious belief does appear to have a sizable impact on family life is fertility. The more conservative people were, the more children they had. In this time of shrinking family size, conservative Christians appear to be heeding the Genesis injunction to "be fruitful and multiply." When one ponders the tremendous impact children have on a marriage (e.g., time and quality of companionship, financial resources and the possible need for additional income, the potential for conflict and growth), this relationship takes on profound significance.[4] We shall explore this relationship in greater detail in Chapter 9.

RELIGIOUS BEHAVIOR

Religious beliefs are in most instances a prerequisite for religious behavior. Therefore we were not particularly surprised to find that the more conservative a person's beliefs, the more often he/she attended church, prayed, and gave money to religious causes. As we explore the extent of religion's impact on marriage, we will examine each of these behaviors in turn.

Church Attendance

"Jim Johnson must be very religious. He attends church every week." This comment typifies the close association in people's minds between the quality of people's religious life and their level of church attendance. This is probably why social scientists seeking to assess religious activity look at levels of church attendance more than anything else.

According to national figures, 40% of the American population attend church on any given Sunday (The Gallup Organization, 1984), which can be compared to the 15% attending church on any given Sunday in England and the 4% to 5% who attend in Sweden (Tomasson, 1970). In significant contrast to both national and international church attendance figures, over 60% of our sample of Christiantowners reported weekly attendance. An additional 20% reported semi-weekly attendance (Figure 4.4). For those inclined to assess religious devotion on this basis, Christiantowners appear quite devout.

Church Attendance and the Marriage Relationship

"Church attendance builds happy marriages." This is the unmistakable message conveyed by one prominent television spot. Although this commercial was no doubt designed to convince people who might think otherwise, the association already runs quite deep in the minds of many Americans. If this thinking is correct, then we should expect to find that couples who attend church regularly have happier marriages, enjoy greater companionship, and experience overall higher levels of marital adjustment than couples who attend church infrequently or not at all.

FIGURE 4.4. Frequency of church attendance

```
===================================================
Level of Attendance        Percent of Individuals Attending [**]
      (number)
===================================================

Every week
    (N=62)        ****************************** 62%

Nearly every week
    (N=21)        ************.21%

At least once a month
    (N=6)         *** 6%
Less often/never
    (N=11)        ****** 11%
---------------------------------------------------
```

From Figure 4.5 it does appear that regular church attenders rate their marriages as slightly happier than less regular attendees. (In analyzing data from the 1987 General Social Survey, we found much the same relationship. See Figure A.2 in Appendix A.) The correspondence we observed is rather small, however. Moreover, for other indicators of marriage quality—companionship and overall adjustment—church attendance seemed to make even less difference.[5,6]

These findings raise an important question. If church attendance is supposed to make such a difference, why isn't there greater difference in the levels of marital happiness, companionship, and adjustment between regular and irregular attenders? We found one clue to why church attendance might appear to make less difference than it actually does in a comment made by one of our respondents, Joan Michaels. When commenting about the most difficult time in her marriage, Joan recalled a period (about three years before our interview) when she and her husband, Ed, were not communicating. In the midst of her search for answers, she started attending church and eventually convinced her husband to attend with her. While indicating that she and her husband were still having problems, she expressed hope that things would improve.

It seems probable that there are others like Joan who attend church in the hope of finding help for a problem marriage. To the extent that this occurs, it stands to appreciably reduce the difference between regular and irregular church attenders in terms of the quality of their respective marriages. Of course, self-selection in church attendance may work the other way. For instance, people with problem marriages who had expected that attending church would help hold their marriages together may lose hope and become less faithful in their attendance.

There are no doubt other factors at work to determine the proportion of people with good or bad, satisfactory or unsatisfactory, marriages who attend church. There is also little doubt that some people's marriages have been helped by becoming active in a church. In our analysis of General Social Survey data (General Social Survey, 1987), we observed that the percentage of couples rating their marriages as "very happy" actually increased slightly, though not significantly, with increased church attendance (Appendix A, Fig-

FIGURE 4.5. Frequency of church attendance and marital happiness

```
=========================================================================

Frequency                 Percent with Very Happy Marriages
(number)                            [**]
-------------------------------------------------------------------------

Weekly (regular)
  (N=62)        ****************************************. 73%

Semi-Weekly
  (N=20)        ***********************************. 65%

Once a Month or Less
  (N=18)        ************************************. 67%

-------------------------------------------------------------------------
```

Spearman Rank Order Correlation for uncollapsed data = .22; p = .01

ure A.3). In terms of the experience of Christiantown couples, however, we can only conclude that with respect to marital well-being, church attendance appears not to make the great difference that some have claimed it does.

The Power of Prayer

Prayer constitutes another significant dimension of religious behavior. Scripture commands it and church leaders endorse it. In light of this strong emphasis, we asked our respondents how often they prayed. Figure 4.6 reveals an interesting pattern: in terms of personal prayer, fully 82% of Christiantowners reported that they pray once a week or more. But when it comes to prayer with a spouse, an entirely different picture emerges. Only 22% indicated that they pray with their spouse once a week or more. Although many Christiantowners indicated that the thing which they find most satisfying about their marriages is companionship, we would have to conclude that this companionship appears not to extend to prayer.

When it comes to the marriage relationship, our findings do not appear to support the assertion that those who pray regularly have better marriages. In fact, the percentage of people with very happy marriages may actually increase with each decrease in prayer frequency (Figure 4.7). The trend is broken only for those who pray rarely or never. Furthermore, we noted the same trend with regard to marital adjustment: as prayer frequency increased, marital adjustment decreased.

Before concluding that prayer may actually cause problems in a marriage, we might consider another possibility. People tend to pray when they feel the greatest need for divine assistance. People whose marriages are unhappy or poorly adjusted—and who have any faith in the power of prayer—pray more often than people whose marriages are in better shape.

So much for prayer apart from the spouse. But what of joint prayer? Much popular wisdom on the subject is reflected in the catchy phrase, "The family that prays together stays together." This aphorism once appeared on numerous signboards across the country. When applied to marriage, the assertion is that couples

FIGURE 4.6. Frequency of individual and joint prayer (excluding prayer to ask blessing on food at mealtime)

Frequency	Percent of Individuals Engaging in Prayer (**)
(number)	Percent of Couples Engaging in Prayer (++)

Daily Prayer
Individuals (n=54) ******************************** 55%
Couples (n=12)   ++++++ 12%

Once a week or more
Individuals (n=27) ****************. 27%
Couples (n=10)   +++++ 10%

Once in a while
Individuals (n=9)   ****. 9%
Couples (n=30)   +++++++++++++++++ 30%

Rarely
Individuals (n=4)   ** 4%
Couples (n=26)   +++++++++++++ 26%

Never
Individuals (n=5)   **. 5%
Couples (n=22)   +++++++++++ 22%

45

FIGURE 4.7. Frequency of prayer as it relates to marital happiness

==

Prayer Frequency   Percent of People With
    (number)   Very happy marriages

Daily   *************************** . 63%
  (n=54)
Weekly   *** 70%
  (n=27)
Occasionally   ** 78%
  (n=9)
Rarely/Never   *************************************** 60%
  (n=10)

----

who engage in prayer together enjoy greater marital stability. The data displayed in Figure 4.8 would appear to support the validity of this slogan. People who pray together as often as once a week are indeed less likely to have considered divorce than those who pray together less often. Yet the frequency of joint prayer, like theological conservatism, turns out to be minimally related to marital companionship and marital adjustment.

Financial Generosity and the Marriage Relationship

The Bible includes much instruction on the proper use of wealth. One story that stands out is recounted in three of the four gospels. A wealthy man approached Jesus and asked what he must do to obtain eternal life. He goes on to explain that he has kept all of God's commandments but asks Jesus what he still lacks. Jesus responds to his question by saying: "If you wish to be complete, go and sell your possessions and give to the poor" (Luke 18:23, New American Standard Bible). Jesus made it clear that this man's willingness to be financially generous was a significant test of his spiritual commitment. This is likely true for others as well. Yet what becomes of the financially generous? Advocates of prosperity theology maintain that those who return both money and firm faith to God will be blessed by health and wealth. We found some evidence of this conviction among our Christiantown respondents. For example, when we asked one woman what she thought would make family life easier, she told us: "Living like dad always advised – give the first 10% of our income to the church." If this logic holds true, then we should find that giving to the church – or to other religious causes – is accompanied by a good marriage.

To get an idea about giving practices, we asked our respondents how frequently they gave a percentage of their income to their church and/or other religious causes. We refrained from using the biblical term "tithe" since we suspected that many people would not be familiar with this concept of giving 10% of one's income to the church. When we examined the relationship between the frequency with which people gave to religious causes and our marital adjustment indicators, we were in for a surprise. As is clear from Figure 4.9, those who make it a regular practice of giving are twice

FIGURE 4.8. Frequency of joint prayer by percent "never" having considered divorce

```
=================================================================

Frequency of joint prayer          Percent having never
        (number)                     considered divorce
-----------------------------------------------------------------

Daily
(n=12)      *********************************. 82%

Once a week or
more (n=10)  ****************************************** 90%

Once in a
while (n=30) *******************************. 69%

Rarely
(n=26)     ***************************** 65%

Never
(n=22)     *******************************. 67%
-----------------------------------------------------------------

Spearman Rank Order Correlation for uncollapsed data = .35; p ≤.01
```

FIGURE 4.9. Regularity of "giving" to religious causes and incidence of above average marital adjustment

===

```
Regularity of "tithing"        Percent with above average
     (number)                     marital adjust  [**]
```

```
Always give
  (n=58)      ************************************. 69%
Generally give
  (n=21)      ***************. 29%
Occasionally or
rarely give
  (n=21)      *****************. 33%
```

Rank Order Correlation = .36; p ≤ .001

as likely to have above average marital adjustment. The same strong relationship was also evident for marital happiness. Those who gave regularly to religious causes were more likely to have very happy marriages than were those who gave less frequently. The same pattern was also evident for divorce. Those who gave money most consistently to the church and/or to religious causes were the least inclined to have ever actively considered divorcing their spouses. Indeed, although a number of our indicators of religious belief or behavior proved to be somewhat related to some aspect of marriage, giving or "tithing" was consistently related to most all of them.

Another possibility is that individuals who give money to religious causes are more generous and that it is generosity (more than tithing to the church) which is reflected in the quality-of-marriage indicators. To check out this possibility, we noted how regularly people gave a percentage of their income to charity. Interestingly, no relationship was apparent between giving to charity and quality of marriage.

The idea that religion favorably affects marital relationships is an appealing one. In this chapter we have examined the impact of religion on marital well-being. In the course of our investigation we found evidence which at least appears to refute some popular notions concerning religion's impact on marriage. For example, we observed that conservatives are more inclined to believe that the Bible teaches wifely subservience, but are just as inclined to have egalitarian marital and sexual relationships as those with less conservative beliefs. Nor did we find any discernible relationship between religious (belief) conservatism and marriage quality.

Religious belief registered perhaps its most dramatic impact on marriage in the form of fertility, a relationship which will be examined in Chapter 9. And of the behavioral measures — church attendance, prayer, and tithing — the latter proved to be the most powerful indicator of marriage quality.

In the upcoming chapters we will occasionally return to the religion factor to assess how this affects or mitigates the impact that other factors have on marriage and family life.

NOTES

1. The Spearman rank order correlation between religious conservatism index score and marital adjustment = .13; p = .09.

2. Not surprising, the correspondence between doctrinal conservatism and agreement concerning biblical teaching on wifely subservience turned out to be somewhat stronger for men than for women.

3. It is possible that people may simply give the "give-and-take" response because it sounds best. Yet our respondents were quite explicit in indicating a distinction between the way they resolved disagreements and the way their parents resolved them. Moreover husbands and wives tended to manifest high levels of agreement on this item. This suggests that our respondents gave serious consideration to this item and attempted to reliably convey the pattern which fit them best. (Chapter 11 contains a further discussion of intergenerational conflict resolution patterns.)

4. Virtually all of our parents indicated that they had completed their family and did not plan to have any more children.

5. The rank order correlation between church attendance and the communication/companionship scale score is .13; between church attendance and the marital adjustment scale score it is .15.)

6. One other form of religious observance did prove to have a somewhat stronger relationship to our indicators of marital well-being. Those who indicated that they regularly engaged in religious observances together in their home tended to have slightly higher marital adjustment and companionship than those who had joint devotions less often or never.

Chapter 5

Sex and Marriage in Christiantown

Because of immoralities, let each man have his own wife, and let each woman have her own husband. Let the husband fulfill his duty to his wife and likewise also the wife to her husband.

—The apostle Paul (1 Cor. 7:2,3,
New American Standard Bible)

After 10 years of marriage, Pam and Toby Clark had concluded that they would be a childless couple. It was not that they did not want children. It was that they could not, or so they thought. Just when they had made an appointment with a social agency to talk about adoption, Pam became pregnant. Then, within a few months after their child was born, Pam found herself pregnant for the second time. That was two years ago. Now, on the occasion of our interview, Pam told us that she was pregnant again, only this time the pregnancy was unplanned and unexpected.

When we spoke with the Clarks, we found them struggling to shoulder the demands that young children place on parents. But it soon became evident that the couple was struggling with another problem—their sexuality. In commenting on their sexual relationship, Pam said, "Toby tends to be the most aggressive one. In fact it sometimes seems like he wants it all the time." When asked what she and her husband disagree about most, Pam unhesitatingly said, "displaying affection." She also noted that she and her husband frequently disagree over sex but nevertheless rated their sex life as "good."

In a separate interview, Toby confirmed what his wife told us about his being the more sexually aggressive of the two. Toby rated their sex life as "fair" and mentioned sex as one of their three areas of greatest disagreement. When asked how he and his wife resolve such disagreements, Toby said that he usually ends up "not getting it." Despite these difficulties, Toby says he and his wife are very much in love. Neither indicated that they had ever considered separation or divorce and both say that if they had it to do over again, they would marry the same person.

The Clarks' high level of marital satisfaction raises some questions. Is there in fact a relationship between sexual expression, fulfillment, and marital well-being? And what factors are closely associated with the expression of sex and the level of sexual satisfaction in marriage? In this chapter we will examine evidence bearing on these questions. The answers are important to an understanding of marital dynamics. Moreover, they have significant implications for professionals interested in facilitating marital well-being.

Several authorities have maintained that sex occupies a primary place in marriage (Masters & Johnson, 1970). Yet certain comments made — or rather not made — by Christiantowners appear to suggest otherwise. For example, when we asked a sample of our respondents what they considered to be the key to marital success, the sexual dimension (like the financial factor) was virtually ignored. And when we inquired about sources of marital satisfaction, again the sexual aspects of marriage were seldom mentioned.

Is the conspicuous absence of references to sex in the context of what Christiantowners view as the requisites for a successful marriage an indication that sex is minimally related to marital satisfaction? After considering the pattern of Christiantown responses to some other questions, this conclusion seems highly questionable. When we examined the relationship between the way people rate their sexual relationship and their level of marital happiness and marital adjustment, an interesting phenomenon became apparent. Each improvement in the sexual relationship is accompanied by a corresponding increase in the percentage of very happy marriages (Figure 5.1). Moreover, much the same relationship is evident between sex rating and overall marital adjustment; the better Christiantowners rate their sexual relationship, the higher their overall score on the marital adjustment index.

Other studies have uncovered a similar correspondence between

FIGURE 5.1. Sex satisfaction and marital happiness

```
================================================================

Rating of Sex
Relationship with        Percentage of Very Happy Marriages
Spouse
 (number)                            [**]
----------------------------------------------------------------


Great
(n=26)    ****************************************** 80%

Good
(n=58)    *********************************** 70%

Fair/Poor
(n=15)    ************** 27%


----------------------------------------------------------------
```

Spearman Rank Order Correlation for uncollapsed data = .25; p = ⩽.04

sexual satisfaction and marital well-being. Drawing from data collected from couples across the United States, Blumstein and Schwartz (1983) found that couples who have the happiest sex lives report less conflict in other areas, such as housekeeping roles and finances. On a more negative note, Burns (1982) found that one of the most frequently given reasons for marital breakdown was sexual incompatibility.

In light of this evidence, it seems apparent that those concerned with the ingredients of a quality marriage need to take the sexual dimension into account. Yet it is not always clear just which way the observed correspondence between sex rating and marital well-being flows. Given the heavy emphasis that sex experts, the media, and popular culture place on sex, we might conclude that sexual satisfaction results in marital happiness and adjustment. Yet if sex is so important for these indicators of marital satisfaction, then our respondents' failure to spontaneously mention sex as the source of marital satisfaction is puzzling. (One might suspect that conservative Christians might be particularly reluctant to make mention of sex; however we noted no discernible difference in this regard between those espousing different religious beliefs.) Given their almost complete silence about sex when stating the sources of their marital satisfaction, we might tentatively suggest that sexual satisfaction is something that flows out of a good marriage rather than something which produces a good marriage. We shall return to this issue in a later section as we deal with husband and wife differences.

Having noted a possibly critical link between sex and marital happiness and adjustment, it seemed appropriate to search out factors which might affect the level of sex satisfaction people experience in marriage. In our search we uncovered factors both internal and external to the marriage itself, which appear to play a significant role in determining sexual satisfaction.

INTERNAL FACTORS AFFECTING SATISFACTION WITH MARITAL SEX

Three internal factors are related to the level of sexual satisfaction. These include marital companionship, sex communication, and sex participation. As we shall see, this latter factor is also associated with marital adjustment.

1. Sexual Satisfaction Improves as Couples Do Things Together

When examining the quality of Christiantown marriages in Chapter 3, we noted the importance Christiantowners place on companionship and the close correspondence between companionship and marital well-being. In light of this correspondence, it seems reasonable to expect that companionship will be closely linked to sexual satisfaction as well. To test this hypothesis, we compared the way in which Christiantowners rate their sexual relationship with their Communication-Companionship Index score. (This index assesses the extent to which couples communicate and participate in activities together.) As is apparent from the data (Figure 5.2) the more positively our respondents rate their sexual relationship, the higher the level of marital communication-companionship.

FIGURE 5.2. How people rate their sexual relationship as it relates to the extent of their communication and companionship (participation in common activities)

===

```
Rating of Sexual                 Percent enjoying high
Relationship                     levels of communication
  (number)                            companionship
```

```
Great Sex
  (n=26)            *************************************. 73%

Good Sex
  (n=58)            ****************************** 60%

Fair/Poor Sex
  (n=15)            ***************. 33%
```

Spearman Rank Order Correlation between rating of sex relationship and Communication-Companionship Index = .55; p = .001

2. As Sexual Communication Improves, Sexual Satisfaction Increases

In a climate in which sex was a taboo subject, St. Clement of Alexandria commented, "It is not right that we are ashamed to call by their names what God was not ashamed to create" (Scanzoni, 1972, p. 4). It is not clear whether St. Clements was referring to discussion of sex in the public or private sphere. But in examining sex and marriage in Christiantown, one thing *is* clear (Figure 5.3): couples who communicate freely about sex have better sexual relationships (Banmen & Vogel, 1985).

This finding raises questions about the wisdom of one spouse — often the husband — assuming that he somehow knows what his wife thinks or wants with respect to sex. How is he to know if he never asks her — or if she never tells him? In such instances, open and honest communication about sex could result in an increased level of satisfaction for both partners (Banmen & Vogel, 1985).

FIGURE 5.3. The relationship between sex communication and sex satisfaction
===

```
Response to the statement:
"My Mate and I
Communicate Freely          Rating of Sex Relationship
About Sex"
-----------------------------------------------------------------


Strongly Agree
(n=38)       ===========53%=============.;**********47%**********.


Agree
(n=52)      xx7%xxx;==============35%=================.;**17%***.


Disagree/
Strongly Disagree
(n=9)       xxxxxxxxxxxxxx67%xxxxxxxxxxxxxxxx.;====22%====;*11%*.



      [**] "great" sex relationship
      [==] "good" sex relationship
      [xx] "poor" or "fair" sex relationship
```

Spearman Rank Order Correlatoin for uncollapsed data = .55; p = ≤.001

a. Sexual Satisfaction Improves with Mutual Participation in the "Act of Marriage"

To assess the extent to which sex is a shared activity, we asked Christiantowners, "Who tends to be more sexually passionate, the wife, the husband, or both about the same?" Just over two-fifths (41%) answered "both about the same," indicating mutual engagement. Another 49% indicated that the husband was more sexually passionate, while the remainder — a mere 10% — indicated that the wife was more passionate.

Traditionally, of course, men have been viewed as the initiators of sexual activity. Recent research indicates that men continue to feel more comfortable than women in initiating sexual behavior (Bahr, 1989, p. 145; Grauerholz & Serpe, 1985). Consequently we were curious to determine whether there was any discernible relationship between the pattern of sexual passion reported by Christiantowners and their level of sexual satisfaction (Figure 5.4). A whopping 91% of those who indicate that both the husband and wife are about equally passionate rate their sex relationship as "good" or "great." It also appears that the highest incidence of "poor" to "fair" sex relationships occurs when the wife is most passionate. (With only a small number of spouses conforming to the "wife most passionate" pattern, this latter observation must be regarded as tentative.) The overall conclusion that emerges is that people rate their sex relationship most positively when sex passion is mutual.

b. Good Marital Adjustment is Closely Associated with Mutual Participation in Sex

A pattern somewhat similar to that between sexual passion and satisfaction became evident when we examined the relationship be-

FIGURE 5.4.* The relationship between sex passion and sex satisfaction

```
=================================================================
Person most
passionate                    Rating of Sex Relationship
(number)
-----------------------------------------------------------------


Wife Most
 (n=10)       xxxxxx30%xxxxxx;======30%======;********40%*********

Husband Most
 (n=47)       xxx19%xxx.;==============64%===============;***17%**.

Both the Same
 (n=39)       x8%x;===========59%==============.;*******33%******.


    [**] "great" sex relationship
    [==] "good" sex relationship
    [xx] "poor" or "fair" sex relationship

-----------------------------------------------------------------
```

Mann-Whitney U between "Both the Same" and "Husband Most" = 708; p = .04
*The distribution of responses within the "Wife Most" = 70-8; p = .04

tween sexual passion and overall marital adjustment (Figure 5.5). Those who indicate a balance in husband and wife passion score much higher in overall marital adjustment. (The percentage of husbands to wives making up this latter group is approximately the same.)

These findings conform quite closely to those of Blumstein and Schwartz (1983, pp. 222-223). Their study found that couples who initiate sex (or refuse sex) on an equal basis are not only more satisfied with their sex lives, but are happier with their overall relationships than are other couples. Mutuality in matters of sex may provide a significant clue as to the well-being of a couple's relationship.

THE IMPACT OF EXTERNAL FACTORS ON MARITAL SEX

All of the above-noted factors point to the complex interplay between sex and marriage. Each provides valuable insights concerning components which have to be considered and possibly dealt with when people encounter problems in their relationships. But what about external factors outside of the marital relationship? Might these also have an impact on the sexual aspect of marriage? In the sections that follow we shall examine the possible influence

FIGURE 5.5. Sex passion and marital adjustment

```
===================================================================

Person Most                Percent of People with Above Average
Sexually Passionate             Marital Adjustment [**]
-------------------------------------------------------------------


Wife Most      *************** 30%
  (n=10)
Husband Most   ************************* 51%
  (n=47)
Both Same      ********************************** 69%
  (n=39)
-------------------------------------------------------------------
```

Kruskal-Wallis H = 5.92; p = .05

that religion and occupation have on the emotionally sensitive sexual sphere of marriage.

Marital Sex and Religion

The early leaders of the Christian church were inclined to view sex with considerable ambivalence if not downright suspicion. As family sociologist John Scanzoni has observed:

> Jerome would not permit married couples to partake of the Eucharist for several days after performing the "bestial act" of intercourse. "A wise man" (he wrote) "ought to love his wife with judgment, not with passion. . . . He who too ardently loves his own wife is an adulterer." (Scanzoni, 1972, p. 4)

After citing similar examples, Scanzoni goes on to observe that this negative image has resulted in an inability for many Christian believers to talk about the subject of sex, even with their spouses.

In recent years there has been an effort to modify this negative imagery and to facilitate better communication about sex, particularly between husband and wife. A number of books have been published proclaiming the legitimacy of sex for Christians. Seminars instructing Christians in the art of obtaining sexual satisfaction have also been introduced. Many of these activities have been motivated by the suspicion that Christians are fraught with disorders which hamper sexual communication and frustrate the experience of sexual satisfaction.

In assessing whether Christians are inclined to have more sexual problems than others, we compared people who hold doctrinally conservative Christian beliefs with those holding less mainstream beliefs. We were curious to see if any systematic difference existed between the two groups in terms of sex communication and sexual satisfaction. We were rather surprised by the findings. An inspection of Figure 5.6 fails to support the notion that orthodox believers are any less inclined to communicate openly about sex. No evidence of a Christian difficulty with sex is apparent, at least with respect to communication.

FIGURE 5.6. How people of different religious beliefs respond to the statement
"My mate and I communicate freely about sex."
```
==================================================================

Christian Beliefs              Rating of Sex Communication
   (number)
------------------------------------------------------------------


Highly Orthodox
   (n=57)

xx 2%; =========================== 54%; ******************** 42%


Less Orthodox/Unorthodox
   (n=42)

xxxxxxxx 16%; ========================= 50%; ****************. 33%


   [**] strongly agree (freely communicate about sex)
   [==] agree
   [xx] disagree/strongly disagree

------------------------------------------------------------------
```
Rank Order Correlation between degree of orthodoxy and rating of sex communi-
cation, using uncollapsed or raw data = .02

But what about sexual satisfaction? Are conservative believers
any less satisfied with their sexual relationships than others? Here
again, our data fail to reveal any difference.[1] Based on the experience of Christiantowners, the notion that orthodox Christians are
less sexually satisfied than others is without foundation.

Marital Sex and Occupation

In contrasting family and occupation, some have described the
former as a realm of "diffuse, enduring solidarity" and the latter as
one of "anxiety, competitiveness, and achievement-orientation"
(Bellah, Madsen, Sullivan, Swindler, & Topton, 1985, p. 87). Different as these two realms are, there is evidence to indicate that a
man's occupational status—a circumstance which largely summa-

rizes the conditions of his work—significantly affects how he relates to his wife (see Chapter 8). But does occupational status have any link to the sexual relationship? To examine this possibility we looked to see if there was any difference in the way husbands of varying occupational status levels rate the sexual aspect of their marriages. A relationship quickly became apparent (Figure 5.7). Christiantown men in high-status occupations rate their sexual relationship with their wives more positively than do men in low-status occupations.

How are these differences to be explained? Since occupational status is somewhat related to income, it may be that income, not occupational status, is the critical factor. Yet our analysis failed to reveal any relationship between income and sex rating. A more viable explanation comes from the work of sociologist Lee Rainwater. Dr. Rainwater found that men in different social classes differ in their approaches to sex. Blue-collar men, for example, are more inclined to stress the physical aspect of sex and to see sex as "a man's privilege and a woman's duty." White-collar men, on the

FIGURE 5.7. How men's occupatoinal status corresponds to their rating of marital sex

```
==========================================================================:

Husband's Occupational
   Status Level
   (number)
--------------------------------------------------------------------

   LOW
   (n=21)
        xxxxxx29%xxxxx.;==============57%=============.;**14%**

   HIGH
   (n=28)
        xx14%xx; ===========50%============;  ********36%*******


   [**] "great" sex relationship
   [==] "good" sex relationship
   [xx] "poor" or "fair" sex relationship
```

Spearman Rank Order Correlation between occupational status level and sex rating for uncollapsed categories = .33; p = ≤ .01

other hand, are inclined to be less aggressive and to stress the relationship aspect of sex (Rainwater, 1964).

Sociologist E. E. LeMasters studied the blue-collar subculture of males by listening and interacting with them in a tavern. After two years of observing, LeMasters made the following observation:

> One can only conclude that for these men sex is sex: it refers to a physical (or organic) experience between a man and a woman. If affection accompanies the sexual act, this is a bonus, but the main ingredient is passion (sexual desire). To these men, sex is a physical need, and sexual satisfaction refers to physical relief, not psychological fulfillment. (LeMasters, 1975, p. 96)

It seems that the contrasts between occupational subcultures reflect a basic difference in the way men of different occupational status groups view sex and women (Gaesser & Whitbourne, 1985).

What about Christiantown husbands? Does their approach to sex vary with their occupational status? When examining differences in sexual expression, there is some indication that it may. Men with lower occupational status tend to be the most passionate in their approach to their wives, whereas men with higher occupational status are more inclined toward a pattern of mutual expression (Figure 5.8). However the difference is small enough that the finding must be regarded somewhat tentatively.

It would be overgeneralizing to imply that sharp distinctions always exist in the subcultures of lower and higher occupational status groupings. However, to the extent that a higher status occupational subculture contributes to a view of women as persons of value in their own right and stresses the primacy of relationships over personal gratification, it may also contribute to greater sexual satisfaction.

We have only begun to examine the impact of occupation on the sexual dimension of marriage. The number of full-time working wives in our sample was not large enough to permit a parallel examination of the impact of wives' occupation on the marriage relationship. But what we have observed thus far strongly indicates that the occupational sphere and the sexual sphere are intertwined to the

FIGURE 5.8. How husband's occupational status level corresponds to expression of sex passion

```
==============================================================================

Occupational
Status Level:
 (number)
-----------------------------------------------------------------------------

  LOW
 (n=21)
         xxxxxxxxxxxxx57%xxxxxxxxxxxxx.;   ==14%==;   *****29%*****.

  HIGH
 (n=26)
         xxxxxx35%xxxxxxx.;  ===15%=.;   ************50%**********

 [xx] husband more passionate
 [==] wife more passionate
 [**] husband and wife equally passionate

-----------------------------------------------------------------------------
```
Kruskal-Wallis H = 2.59; p = ⩽.11

extent that experience in one has implications for experience in the other. As we shall see in Chapters 7 and 8, the occupational experience is linked in a significant way to other aspects of marriage as well.

SEXUAL SATISFACTION AND MARRIAGE QUALITY: HUSBAND-WIFE DIFFERENCES

In comparing the responses of Christiantown husbands and wives, certain differences became apparent. These differences likely reflect a variation in the way the two sexes perceive marriage as evidenced by the stress they place on certain aspects of the marriage relationship. Earlier we noted the close correspondence between marriage quality and sexual satisfaction. After analyzing separately the relationship between companionship and sexual satisfaction for husbands and for wives, a difference became apparent. Companionship, we found, has more to do with the sexual satisfaction of wives than of husbands.[2] When we did a similar analysis for marital happiness, a somewhat different pattern became apparent (Figure 5.9). In contrast to companionship, marital happiness has more to do with sexual satisfaction for husbands than it does for wives.

The causal relationship between these two measures of marriage quality and sexual satisfaction is not obvious from our data. Yet some writers have insisted that, to the extent that a difference between the two sexes exists, men approach love through sex while women approach sex through love (Ehrmann, 1959; Wiese, 1972). Based on our data for Christiantowners, we might tentatively suggest that sexual satisfaction is more important for the marital happiness of husbands, whereas companionship is more important to the sexual satisfaction of wives.

From the data presented in this chapter it is apparent that marriage quality is intimately tied to the sexual dimension. Although

FIGURE 5.9. Husbands' ratings of the sex relationship have more to do with their marital happiness than wives' ratings of the relationship
```
==================================================================

Rating of Sex                  Very Happy Marriages
Relationship

Great Sex
  (n=13)        xxxxxxxxxxxxxxxxxxx 92% xxxxxxxxxxxxxxxxxxxxxx

  (n=13)        *************** 69% **************:

Good Sex
  (n=27)        xxxxxxxxxxxxxx 74% xxxxxxxxxxxxxxxxxx

  (n=31)        ************* 68% ****************

Fair/Poor Sex
  (n=10)        xxxxx 30% xxxxx

  (n=5)         *** 20% **

[xx] Husbands reporting very happy marriages
[**] Wives reporting very happy marriages

------------------------------------------------------------------
```
Spearman Rank Order Correlation between sex rating and marital happiness rating for men = .49; correlation for women = .35; cell frequencies were too small to provide an adequate test of group differences.

male and female differences exist, the sexes still have more similarities than differences. Despite the assertions that are sometimes heard concerning the supposed problems Christians have with sex, conservative Christians enjoy sex and communicate about it as much as less conservative believers. Several factors appear to affect the quality of the sexual relationship, including sexual participation, sexual communication, and marital companionship. We have also begun to see how one's occupation can affect the sexual relationship. Further light will be shed on this matter as we consider data presented in the forthcoming chapters on income and employment.

NOTES

1. It could be that Christians are inclined to expect less in the way of sexual satisfaction from a relationship and, expecting less, are more easily satisfied. This possibility must await further examination.

2. The correlation between sexual satisfaction and marital happiness for husbands = .49; for wives the correlation is .32. The correlation between sexual satisfaction and the Communication/Companionship score for husbands is .26; for wives it is .35.

Chapter 6

Money and Marriage

For the love of money is a root of all sorts of evil.

—I Timothy 6:10, The New Testament
(*New American Standard Bible*)

For the son of a butcher, Ralph Michaels has been quite successful. After graduating from high school, Ralph married his high school sweetheart and started working as a clerk in a local bank. Now, after seventeen years of marriage, he is a successful bank executive earning a comfortable $50,000 annual income. Yet despite his high salary and secure position, Ralph insists on retaining total control over the family finances, doling out only so much as his wife Roberta needs for groceries and other household necessities. Although the majority of Christiantowners indicated that they have a high degree of trust in their mate, Ralph said that he trusts his wife in some things but not in others. Roberta, who functions as a full-time housewife, told us that she and her husband rarely discuss major financial expenditures. But when asked about the area of greatest disagreement in her marriage, she unhesitatingly responded, "Money."

We cannot say for sure whether distrust and disagreement over money was the source of the Michaels' low level of marital happiness and adjustment. Yet it is clear from other studies that a great deal of marital dissatisfaction arises from conflicts over money (Saxton, 1980, p. 547). In this chapter we will examine the impact of financial companionship, income, and money management on the marriage relationships of Christiantowners.

Before proceeding further, it is important to point out that of the

67

fifty wives we interviewed, only half were employed and of these, only 36% were employed full-time. Thus in most instances the husband was the primary income earner. This should not diminish the contribution of unemployed wives. According to one calculation (Mackey, 1985), the value of a wife's unpaid work at home is worth about two-thirds of a family's income.

FINANCIAL COMPANIONSHIP

To help assess our couples' approach to finances, we examined their responses to three key questions. The first dealt with a special situation. "If husband should receive extra income from a special project, would this be: (a) his to use as he saw fit, (b) the wife's to use as she saw fit, (c) both yours and your spouse's? Eighty-five percent of our respondents selected the last response, indicating that they regarded extra income as the common property of both. We pursued this issue further by asking working wives whether their income was theirs to use as they chose, the husband's to use as he chose, or whether it belonged to both the husband and the wife. Again a similar pattern of sharing appeared, with over 80% of working wives indicating that their earnings belonged to both spouses.

As a third means of assessing financial companionship, we inquired whether our married respondents discussed major financial expenditures with their spouses. In this instance 93% indicated that they always discussed such expenditures.

Up to this point it appeared that financial discord is virtually unknown for the majority of Christiantowners. In fact it began to seem that, although other studies found strong evidence of conflict over money, Christiantowners constituted a notable exception. Before settling on this conclusion, we thought it best to examine the areas in which our respondents indicated frequent disagreement. Suddenly a different picture emerged. Of those areas of disagreement noted, money and finances were mentioned more frequently than any other area. (Recreation and politics came in a distant second and third.) This need not imply that Christiantowners are forever fighting over finances, but it does indicate that a high degree of financial companionship does not preclude such disagreement.

Why So Much Disagreement Over Finances?

Why, in light of their ready inclination to share income and financial decisions, are finances mentioned as the most common source of disagreement? One plausible explanation arises from the subjective nature of material desires. Such desires are subjective precisely because of the difficulty of securing any broad consensus concerning their importance. Consequently, a wife may feel that she desperately "needs" the latest home entertainment sound system or a husband may set his heart on the latest lap-top computer despite the fact that both have been getting along rather well with older equipment. A recurring conflict experienced by one Christiantown couple became evident in a comment made by the wife. After "getting by" for years with their used Buick, Margaret Richards was convinced that the family needed a new car. "Every time I take that car out I'm afraid that it'll break down and I won't make it back home." "Besides," Margaret added, "that old car parked in front of our driveway is an embarrassment to the neighborhood. But every time I bring up the subject, Mike (her husband) just says that the car's in 'sound mechanical condition' and that we have better things to spend our money on. Mike works on that old car all the time. Sometimes I suspect that he thinks more of that car than he does of me."

Subjective needs come from a variety of sources. The media serves to cultivate such desires. As Harvey Cox (1985) observes in his book, *The Seduction of the Spirit*, the media tells us where our shortcomings lie—our cars are unsafe, our weight is unsightly, our clothes make us undesirable, unattractive, and unsuccessful. The media stresses that many, if not most, of our shortcomings are due to old, inadequate, and inferior consumer goods. It teaches us that the key to happiness, security, and success lies in discovering and securing the smart, right, new, and often expensive product.

The media can scarcely be held responsible for all subjective material "needs" and all the conflicts these needs produce. Divergent backgrounds and experiences give rise to divergent needs. The problem that Mr. and Mrs. Richards were having over their car may have arisen from their different role models. Margaret's parents may have always bought new cars, furniture, and other big-ticket items, while Mike's might have been content to settle for used "bargains."

A similar difference of opinion concerning material needs arises from what sociologists refer to as divergent socialization between the sexes. Although things may be changing, in past generations girls, while growing up, tended to find that they got attention from looking pretty. Eventually they concluded that clothes were the "props" necessary for being admired and appreciated. The wife who pleads with her husband that she needs a new dress is likely reflecting this sort of socialization. Men, of course, were once socialized to "need" certain goods of their own—but these goods tended to be ones which helped them to affirm their male identity, cars and hot rods are a case in point.

Conditioned needs cannot easily be separated from those which emerge from the various groups people use to measure their consumption. We have all heard of the desire to keep up with the Joneses. A husband's desire to keep up with the fellows at his health club or a wife's desire to dress as well as the other women in the office are merely manifestations of this same phenomenon.

Whatever their source, subjective desires frequently fail to find legitimacy in the mind of one's spouse. When this happens, hurt feelings, misunderstandings, and conflict will occur, even among couples who endeavor to blend their incomes and share in financial decision-making.

How Are Family Income and Marital Well-Being Related?

In considering our findings thus far, it might have occurred to the reader that disagreement over finances may actually be a function of income. It seems logical to expect that those with limited income are under considerable pressure to stretch their funds as far as possible and that this pressure results in disagreement over finances. Yet when we checked for a possible correspondence between the amount of family income and the extent of financial disagreement, we found little if any evidence of a relationship. Perhaps our findings would have been different had our community included more low-income families. While considering the effects of income, it occurred to us that this variable might affect the marriage relationship in some other way.

To help probe the deeper issues of marriage, we posed a number of open-ended questions to a subset of our sample. In our lead-off question, we asked approximately half of our sample of husbands and wives what they regarded as the key to marital success. Interestingly, not one of them made any reference to money. In fact any mention of materialistic considerations was, with one exception, wholly lacking. References to finances did surface, however, in their responses to other questions. For example, when we asked Christiantowners if they could think of anything that would make their family life easier, references to such things as job security and paying off debts appeared. In her response to this question, one woman told us quite directly that the thing which would make her family life easier would be "more cash." And when we inquired about what things tended to worry or concern our respondents most, fully one-third mentioned financial matters. Confronted with this evidence, we began to suspect that our respondents' failure to link financial factors to marital success might be due to a somewhat romantic and unrealistic approach to marriage. We pursued our suspicion first by examining the correspondence between total income and reports of marital happiness. Here a definite difference emerged between husbands and wives (Figure 6.1). While increments in family income tend to be accompanied by increases in marital happiness ratings for wives, the correspondence is practically nonexistent for husbands.

The same trend is even more apparent for our composite measure of marital adjustment (Figure 6.2). Every increase in income level is accompanied by an increased incidence of high marital adjustment for wives, but not for husbands. In this case the percentage of women with above-average marital adjustment is twice as great for wives in the highest income group as it is for wives in the lowest group.

In the midst of our analysis, we learned that the 1987 General Social Survey, a national sample of Americans conducted by the National Opinion Research Center in Chicago, contained questions on both income and marital happiness. We were curious to find out whether a similar pattern would appear. We were fascinated to dis-

FIGURE 6.1. Total family income by level of marital happiness for women

```
===========================================================
Annual Income               Percentage rating their
Level in Dollars              Marriage as Very Happy
(number)
-----------------------------------------------------------
Under 25,000
   (15)     ************************** 60%

From 25 to 29,999
   (10)       ********************* 50.0%

From 30 to 39,999
   (13)     ********************************** 76.9%

40,000 and above
   (12)     ***********************************. 83.3%
-----------------------------------------------------------
```

Spearman Rank Order Correlation for uncollapsed data = .25; p ≤ .04

FIGURE 6.2. Total family income by level of marital satisfaction for women

===

Annual Income   Percent with Above Average
Level in Dollars   Marital Adjustment
(number)

Under 25,000
(15)   ********************. 33.3%

From 25 to 29,999
(10)   ************************ 40.0%

From 30 to 39,999
(13)   ***************************************. 61.5%

40,000 and above
(12)   ***. 66.7%

Spearman Rank Order Correlation for uncollapsed data = .30; p ≤ .02

73

cover that the General Social Survey data reflected the same positive correspondence between income level and marital happiness for women but, as in the case of Christiantowners, little relationship for men (Appendix A, Table A.4).

Before concluding that wives' marital happiness and satisfaction are determined by income level, we thought it best to examine the possibility that both might be due to some third factor, and that the relationship is actually spurious. Both occupational status and education are related to income. Moreover we found that a husband's education is positively related to a wife's feeling of being understood by him and that this feeling of being understood is in turn associated with overall marital adjustment. Yet the relationship between income and wives' marital adjustment persists even after controlling for these variables. (A wife's employment status did not make a difference; marital well-being continued to be related to income for both employed and unemployed wives.) It appears, then, that income does indeed affect wives' sense of marital well-being.

Why, we wondered, should income prove to be such a good predictor of marital well-being for wives but not for husbands? Our first thought was that it might have something to do with money management. National surveys indicate that the task of money management falls more often to wives than to husbands and our Christiantown couples were no exception. It is possible, we reasoned, that in the course of processing the bills, women may become more concerned about financial matters and this in turn may adversely affect their marriage. Yet our data failed to support this notion. In fact, when concern over insufficient funds was expressed, more often than not the funds were being managed by the husband. (We'll consider the impact of money management on marriage in greater detail a bit later.)

A second possible explanation involves the way in which married people typically allocate responsibilities. In Western culture the husband, in his traditional breadwinner role, has functioned as an income producer while his wife, in her domestic role, has been the primary income consumer. Some realignment of these roles has occurred as women have followed their husbands into the work force. Yet while today's couples tend to hold more egalitarian attitudes concerning the allocation of work than have past generations, evidence also indicates that these attitudes are seldom reflected in actual behavior (Condran & Bode, 1982; Erickson, Yancey, & Erickson, 1979; Stafford, Backman, & diBonda, 1977). Yet today's wives and mothers still do the bulk of the grocery shopping while remaining primarily responsible for taking the children for their shots, and in other ways securing the goods and services needed by their families (Coverman & Sheley, 1986; Ferber, 1982.) Consequently wives must continually be concerned with stretching available income to cover the cost of caring for the family.

The availability of labor saving devices, the presence of a second car, and the quality of neighborhood, house, and furnishings are all largely determined by the size of a family's income. And for many Christiantown couples, it is the wife, as primary "keeper of the hearth," who spends much of her time living with what the family income has provided. Since her husband, in most instances, still assumes the role of primary breadwinner, it seems plausible that a wife's satisfaction with her husband will be influenced at least in part by how well he fills this provider role.

Does Religion Mitigate the Impact of Income?

Christianity has had a strong injunction against seeking satisfaction through material consumption. Therefore it would seem that wives who hold to conservative Christian beliefs would be less affected by family income. However from the data in Figure 6.3 it is apparent that the relationship between income and marital satisfaction persists irrespective of how conservative a woman's religious beliefs. It appears that conservative beliefs in themselves fail to exempt wives from the effects of income on the marriage relationship.

MONEY MANAGEMENT

Andrew and Darla Terry have spent the eleven years of their marriage working at what they term "a 100% relationship." Both seek to share their lives with the other in as many ways as possible — in their friendships, their religious life, and their leisure time

FIGURE 6.3. Income and marital adjustment scores for women holding conservative Christian beliefs

```
=====================================================================
Total Annual                    Percent with Above Average
   Income                            Marital Adjustment
  (number)
---------------------------------------------------------------------
Less than $30,000
     (n=16)        *********************************** 50%

$30,000 or more
     (n=16)        ************************************************** . 75%

---------------------------------------------------------------------
```

Kruskal-Wallis H - 2.01; p = ≤.15

activities. Both expressed a high degree of trust in the other and both maintained that they keep no secrets from the other. When it comes to finances, the Terrys reported sharing the responsibility equally.

In this latter respect the Terrys are a clear exception. Although many of our couples enjoyed a high degree of marital companionship, few Christiantowners (a mere 9%) reported that they shared equally the task of managing the money. In most instances, it was either the husband or the wife who managed the money (Figure 6.4), with "wife always" being the prevailing pattern. Perhaps the reason why few couples share this task equally is largely pragmatic. Unless one person assumes major responsibility, there may be risk of slip-ups in paying the bills on time, etc.

What Determines Who Manages the Money?

With so many varied notions concerning the appropriate person to manage the finances, we explored possible bases for selecting a particular pattern of management. One possible influence includes religion.

In Chapter 4 we examined a stereotype which is frequently applied to the marriages of conservative Christians, namely, that they tend to be husband-dominant. Several Christian leaders have courted this image by insisting that the wife be properly submissive to her husband. When it comes to money management, such spokesmen maintain that the money management decision should be determined by gender, with the husband taking charge. Occasionally their logic rests on the belief in a hierarchical order ordained by God in which the wife falls under the authority of the husband as he in turn falls under the authority of God. Sometimes the argument is rooted in the supposed nature of women whom God did not design (or intend) to withstand the pressures of financial concern (e.g., Christenson, 1970). In light of such instruction, we were curious to learn whether religious belief had any discernible bearing on who manages the money. As it turns out, however, the pattern is surprisingly symmetrical for this group, with the largest percentages (roughly a third in each instance) opting for either a "husband always" or a "wife always" pattern (Figure 6.5). With

FIGURE 6.4. Who keeps track of the money and the bills?

Money Management Pattern	Frequency/Percent
Husband Always	20
Husband More than Wife	24
Husband & Wife Exactly the Same	9
Wife More than Husband	15
Wife Always	32

Total =	100

FIGURE 6.5. Money management arrangement used by people scoring at the highest level of Christian conservatism

Manager	Percent Employing	Number
Husband Always	32.3%	10
Husband More than Wife	12.9%	4
Husband & Wife the Same	9.7%	3
Wife More than Husband	12.9%	4
Wife Always	32.3%	10
	100 %	31

so little difference between the patterns of money management practices of those holding highly conservative and those holding less conservative beliefs, we must conclude that the husband dominant stereotype once again fails for lack of support.

Another factor which some suppose to determine money management patterns is wife employment. Family sociologists have observed that a wife's influence in marriage increases according to the extent of her financial contribution (Blood & Wolfe, 1960; Scanzoni & Scanzoni, 1988). According to this logic, we ought to find that working women, by virtue of their financial contribution, tend to assume the money management role more often than nonworking women. When we compared the incidence of money management for Christiantown wives who worked full-time with those who worked less or who were not employed, we noted that those in the former group were much more likely to report that they usually or always managed the family's money (Figure 6.6). (We did not determine the actual number of hours that part-time employees invested in their work.) Perhaps we are seeing a partial affirmation of the truth expressed in the old adage, "money belongs to the one who earns it, not to the one who spends it."

Is Money Management a Privilege or an Obligation?

If managing family finances were simply another chore to be done like keeping house or caring for the kids, we might expect that full-time housewives—who some would suggest have more time available than their employed-wife counterparts—would assume this task more often than their employed husbands. On the other hand, employed wives would seemingly be glad to give this chore over to their husbands. But if managing the finances constitutes a privilege—perhaps allowing the manager more input concerning income disbursements—then we should expect that employed women will use their influence as income-producers to secure this role for themselves. Our findings are most in line with this latter interpretation. In addition to their employment, working wives typically remain responsible for major domestic tasks such as shopping, cooking, laundering, and caring for the children. Consequently what we

FIGURE 6.6. Wife's employment status by incidence of wife's money management

```
===================================================================

Wife's Employment              Percent in Which
     Status                     Wife Always
    (number)                      Manages
-------------------------------------------------------------------

Housewife
  (n=46)    ********************** 26.1%
Part-Time
  (n=22)    ****************************. 31.3%
Full-Time
  (n=18)    ******************************************** 50%
-------------------------------------------------------------------
```

Kruskal-Wallis H = 3.34; p = ≤.19

may be seeing is an effort to honor the principle that the person who contributes most enjoys the greater privilege.

What Is the Consequence of Money Management?

Which pattern of money management relates most closely to good marital adjustment? There is considerable disagreement — even among those writing for primarily Christian audiences, about whether money matters should be gender-linked. For example, Christenson (1970, pp. 44-45) suggests that adverse consequences will befall those marriages in which the wife manages the finances, whereas Wiese and Steinmetz (1972, p. 147) believe that the husband-dominant pattern of money management is fraught with danger.

Which position comes closer to the truth? It would appear from our sample that couples who follow the husband-dominant pattern of money management are not as well-adjusted as those who share the responsibility or allocate it to the wife (Figure 6.7). Why the difference? We cannot say for sure, but we suspect that husbands who control finances tend to usurp this role for themselves and the wife-management pattern more often results from mutual consensus.

ARE CHRISTIANTOWNERS MATERIALISTIC?

Materialism tends to convey negative connotations. People are not supposed to base their happiness on material consumption. This may be one reason why none of our couples mentioned finances and were disinclined to refer to material considerations when answering our interview question concerning the keys to marital success. To give them the benefit of the doubt, it is entirely possible that Christiantown couples, like many others, are not conscious of the subtle impact that material circumstance has on marriage. Yet drawing from the significant correspondence we found for women between total family income and marital happiness and adjustment, it appears that the importance of the material situation in which wives find themselves should not be underrated.

The manner in which money is handled and the way in which

FIGURE 6.7. Money Manager by Marital Adjustment Level

```
=================================================
Money Manager          Percent with Above Average
  (number)                 Marital Adjustment
-------------------------------------------------
Husband Always
  (n=20)         ******************** 40.0%
Husband More
  (n=24)         ***************************** 58.3%
Husband & Wife Same
  (n=9)          ********************************* . 66.7%
Wife More
  (n=15)         ************************************** . 73.3%
Wife Always
  (n=32)         ********************************* 65.6%

-------------------------------------------------
```

Rank Order Correlation between money manager and marital adjustment score = .27; p = ≤.01

financial decisions are made is an important factor in the marriage relationship. Although Christiantowners typically share in financial decisions and enjoy a high level of financial companionship, money is still the most frequent topic of disagreement. Moreover, finances turn out to be strongly linked to a wife's marital happiness and adjustment. In the next chapter we turn our attention to a related area of concern, the impact of a husband's employment on the marriage relationship.

Chapter 7

Earning a Living:
The Impact of Husband's Employment

What you do is who you are.

— Anthony Campolo

By most standards, Dan Graham represents a self-made man. Early in his life Dan's father, a high school drop-out, instilled in his son the idea that if he could just get an education, the sky was the limit. After two years of putting himself through college, Dan met and married his wife Susan. Dan was able to finish the last two years of college with the help of his working wife. After graduating with a bachelor's degree in business, Dan got a job with a small accounting firm. At the low end of his corporate ladder, he was saddled with the work that his superiors in the firm threw his way. Today Dan has secured a senior accountant position in another firm and still puts in long hours at the office and with his clients. Susan, who had expected to see more of her husband after he completed college, is trying to reconcile herself to the idea that Dan is in a very competitive occupation and that his practice of investing long hours on the job is not likely to change. Susan confided to us that she missed her husband and her voice conveyed a certain weariness. While Dan rated his marriage as very happy, Susan gave it a mid-range (average) rating.

The investment that many men make in their occupational roles is so great that it has prompted some social scientists to maintain that a man's work determines his very identity. Yet the nature and extent of work's impact on the marriage relationship has become a matter of some debate. In this chapter we will seek to determine whether a man's occupational experience does in fact have a discernible impact on marriage, and the nature of this impact. But before we pursue this issue, it will be helpful to profile the kinds of occupations in which Christiantowners are involved. With the assistance of Treisman's (1977, Appendix A) occupational prestige scale, we assigned each of our respondents a prestige value based on his occupation. Since we inquired about the kind of work that fathers were in while our respondents were growing up, we were also able to generate a similar profile for fathers. By juxtaposing these two profiles, the extent of intergenerational mobility quickly becomes apparent (Figure 7.1).

The bulk of our respondents' fathers fall between levels three and four on the index. These ranks are filled with truck drivers, carpen-

FIGURE 7.1.* Prestige ratings for Fathers' and Sons' Occupations

```
=======================================================
Prestige Level
-------------------------------------------------------
Low
   Level Two      Fathers = (2.0%)
                  Sons    * (2.0%)

   Level Three    Fathers ============== (28.0%)
                  Sons    *** (6.0%)

   Level Four     Fathers ============== (28.0%)
                  Sons    **** (10.0%)

   Level Five     Fathers ========= (18.0%)
                  Sons    *********** (24.0%)

   Level Six      Fathers ==== (8.0%)
                  Sons    ****************** (38.0%)

   Level Seven    Fathers ===== (10.0%)
                  Sons    ********* (18.0%)
High
-------------------------------------------------------
```

Kruskal-Wallis H = 22.47; p = ≤.001
*Three of the fathers' occupations and one son's were not codeable due to insufficient information.

ters, machinists, farmers, bookkeepers, bank tellers, and police-
men — occupations which are, for the most part, blue-collar and
semi-skilled. The bulk of the sons, however, occupy ranks five
through seven.[1] In these ranks we find the teachers, CPAs, engi-
neers, physicists, pharmacists, market analysts, merchandisers, and
corporate managers — occupations which make up the professional
class. For a few Christiantown husbands the means to upward mobility and higher occupational status has been sheer physical labor,
but advanced education has been the primary qualifier. A full 80%
hold college degrees and over 40% of these have secured postgradu-
ate degrees.

HOW DOES A HUSBAND'S WORK AND CAREER
AFFECT HIS MARRIAGE?

We have all heard stories about men who, in their striving for
success, have so thrown themselves into their work that their marriages became sorely strained. The Grahams, whose case was reviewed at the outset, represent one such instance.

A characteristic of many high status jobs is that they are not
structured on a 9-to-5 basis. Deadlines, committee assignments,
honorary board memberships, and a host of other circumstances
often add up to long days and occasionally long weekends on the
job and away from wife and family. We heard a number of complaints from both husbands and wives about how much time the
husband's work demands. Books such as Greiff and Munter's
Tradeoffs: Executive, Family, and Organizational Life (1981) and
Seidenberg's *Corporate Wives — Corporate Casualties?* (1973) call
attention to the trappings which can accompany occupational
achievement. No doubt many a family has paid a bitter price for a
husband's accomplishments at work. But there is reason to suspect
that a bright side exists. It has to do with the feeling of pride and
success that comes from holding a high status position. Sociologist
Tony Campolo has observed that the question most frequently directed to men is, "What do you do?" To this question, the typical
response is, "I am a plumber," "I am an engineer," or "I am a
senior accountant at . . ." What is significant about the response,
says Campolo (1984), is that when men are asked what they do,

they answer in terms of who they are. The kind of work men do, Campolo concludes, determines their identity and, because of the status attached to that work or position, their dignity as well. In other words, high prestige occupations bring positive recognition which psychologically equates to a positive self-image and positive mental attitude.

How does this affect the marriage relationship? Psychologists have observed that a favorable self-concept contributes to good interpersonal relationships. Since marriage represents one such relationship, to the extent that high status makes for a positive self-image, it also contributes to a good marriage and to overall marital adjustment.

TWO CONFLICTING ARGUMENTS

Thus, we have two conflicting lines of logic: one which predicts a decline in marital adjustment with increased occupational status and one which predicts an increase. After tabulating the results, it is apparent (Figure 7.2) that low occupational status does not bode well for the marriage relationship of Christiantowners. However since this is only true of the lowest levels and since the number of Christiantowners falling into these categories of occupational status is quite small, we must remain tentative in our suggestion that improvements in occupational status are accompanied by improvements in the marriage relationships. But what we can say with certainty is that, in terms of marital adjustment, low occupational status is not compensated for by a better marriage relationship. Nor is there any evidence to indicate that for the majority of Christiantowners, holding down a high status job is detrimental to the marriage relationship.

WHAT ABOUT WIVES?

Is there any reason to expect that the sacrifices often required of women whose husbands hold down high status positions is offset by other gains? It may be that wives whose husbands enjoy high occupational status come to view their husbands with the same positive regard that society has conferred on them. It may also be that hus-

FIGURE 7.2. Occupational status by husband's marital adjustment

```
===============================================
Status Level                 Percent With Above
  (number)                   Average Marital Adjustment
-----------------------------------------------
Low = levels 2 to 4
  (n=9)          *****************. 33.3%

Moderate = level 5
  (n=12)         *****************************. 58.3%

High = level 6
  (n=19)         *****************************. 57.9%

Very High = level 7
  (n=9)          ****************************. 55.6%
-----------------------------------------------
Kruskal-Wallis H = 1.71; p = ≤.64
```

89

bands who have won high occupational status manifest an air of confidence and optimism and that their wives respond positively to these qualities. On the other hand, husbands who have failed to achieve such status, to quote comedian Rodney Dangerfield, "don't get no respect."

A number of reasons probably combine to account for the relationship which emerges in Figure 7.3. But one thing seems clear: for Christiantown wives, below-average marital adjustment is much more apparent when their husbands enjoy only low or moderate occupational status.

The relationships depicted in Figure 7.3 do not seem to be particularly unique to Christiantowners. In their study of over 700 wives living in the Detroit area, Blood and Wolfe (1960, p. 253) found that wives' marital satisfaction closely paralleled increments in their husbands' occupational status.[2]

HOW IMPORTANT IS A HUSBAND'S JOB SATISFACTION?

Ordinarily job satisfaction and occupational status tend to go hand-in-hand. Yet we found that some Christiantown husbands with high status positions registered low or moderate job satisfaction while others in positions of lesser status were quite satisfied with their work. These exceptions, we felt, warranted giving special attention to the impact of job satisfaction on marriage.[3]

As in the case of occupational status, there are contrasting lines of reasoning concerning the impact of job satisfaction on marital well-being. According to one line of reasoning, job satisfaction contributes to good mental health and, due to a spill-over effect, this has a positive effect on the marriage relationship. Conversely, poor work satisfaction contributes to poor mental health which in turn infects the marriage relationship. We will henceforth refer to this as the spill-over hypothesis.

If people find this hypothesis appealing, it may be because it conforms to their own experiences. But there is another line of reasoning which predicts the opposite effect. Derived from George Homans' (1961) exchange theory, we will refer to it as the compensatory needs hypothesis. The rationale is that work satisfaction is

FIGURE 7.3. * Husband's occupational status and wife's marital adjustment

```
=======================================================

Status Level                      Percent with Above
(number)                         Average Marital Adjustment
-------------------------------------------------------

Low = levels 2 to 4
   (n=7)              ****************. 28.57%
Moderate = level 5
   (n=13)             *******************. 38.5%
High = level 6
   (n=20)             *********************************. 65.0%
Very High = level 7
   (n=9)              **********************************. 66.67%

-------------------------------------------------------
```

Kruskal-Wallis H for levels 2 to 5 compared to levels 6 and 7 = 4.34; p = ≤.04
*The observed relationship between husband's occupational status and wife's marital adjustment does not seem to reflect husband's education. For wives who's husbands hold graduate degrees, the correspondence between husband's occupational status remains sizable (Spearman r = .31).

proportional to the level of recognition or "positive stroking" a man receives through his work. But a person can use only so much stroking and after a husband has his quota of "I love you's" met at work, he is less inclined to seek them at home. In effect, then, work satisfaction leads to less need for marital interaction and the resulting decline in interaction adversely affects marital well-being.

By the same logic, the husband with low job satisfaction is receiving less stroking from his work. Failing to have his quota of "I love you's" filled in the work place, he turns to his wife. From the standpoint of this compensatory needs hypothesis, poor job satisfaction actually contributes to greater marital interaction. Quite simply, rather than putting all his eggs into the career basket, the husband with low job satisfaction puts more of his eggs into the marriage basket. If the strategy is successful, poor work satisfaction may actually contribute to a good marriage.

We were first alerted to the possible importance of the compensatory function of marriage by a comment one woman made when indicating who was most sexually passionate. She observed that since her husband began having problems with his new supervisor, he had become much more passionate toward her. Could it be that a husband's occupational satisfaction affects his bedroom behavior? We decided to explore this possibility by comparing husbands' job satisfaction with those whose wives rated them as more sexually passionate. What we found appears to lend support to the compensatory needs hypothesis (Figure 7.4).

It seems plausible that job satisfaction affects marital interaction in other areas as well. To check this out we incorporated our index of communication and companionship. This index measures the extent to which husbands and wives communicate and share activities together. If poor job satisfaction motivates a husband to invest more effort in his marriage, then we should find that communication-companionship scores actually increase with decreased job satisfaction. In fact we found little evidence of this (Figure 7.5). Only a minority of husbands with poor to fair occupational satisfaction enjoy high communication-companionship, and the percentage increases with each correspondingly higher level of job satisfaction. Apparently husbands with poor work satisfaction relate to their wives sexually but not conversationally.

FIGURE 7.4. Husband's occupational satisfaction by wives' rating of husbands' sex passion

```
===============================================================

Occupational Satis-      Number      Percent Indicating Husband
faction Level                        Most Sexually Passionate
---------------------------------------------------------------

Fair to Poor
  (n=15)               ******************. 33%

Good
  (n=29)               ******************************** 66.7%

---------------------------------------------------------------
```

Kruskal-Wallis H = 4.04; p = ≤.05

FIGURE 7.5. Husband's Occupational Satisfaction by Husbands' Communication-Companionship Scores

==

Occupational satis- faction Level (number)	Percent with High (above average) Communication- Companionship Scores

----

High
(n=14)   ** 71.4%

Moderate
(n=17)   *********************************** 64.7%

Poor to Fair
(n=15)   ************************** 46.7%

Spearman Rank Order Correlation for ungrouped data = .27; p = ≤ .08
Kruskal-Wallis H = 1.99; p = ≤.37

94

We gained further insight into the situation when we examined how husbands with varying levels of job satisfaction feel about the feedback they get from their wives after sharing their troubles with them. Only one-third of the husbands with poor to fair job satisfaction reported feeling much better. In contrast, well over half of the husbands with moderate to high occupational satisfaction reported feeling much better after sharing their troubles.

Evidence by Barling (1984) suggests that the adverse effects of poor job satisfaction among husbands extends to their wives. This seems to be the case for Christiantowners. In fact, wives and husbands both register lower levels of marital happiness and satisfaction as the husband's occupational satisfaction decreases.

As we have seen, Christiantown husbands enjoy a considerably higher occupational status than their fathers did. But high status jobs can have varying consequences. On the one hand, marriage and family life occasionally suffers when a husband and father over-invests himself in his career by working long hours at a high pressure job. For many Christiantowners, however, high status positions are associated with correspondingly high levels of marital happiness and adjustment. Because dissatisfaction with one's work can occur at any status level, this factor must be taken into consideration when assessing the impact of work on marital well-being.

With growing numbers of women finding employment outside the home, it is appropriate to consider also the potential impact of women's work on marital well-being. It is to this topic that we turn in the next chapter.

NOTES

1. Three of the father's occupations and one son's were not codeable due to insufficient information.

2. The observed relationship between husband's occupational status and wife's marital adjustment does not seem to reflect husband's education. For wives whose husbands hold graduate degrees, the correspondence between husband's occupational status remains sizable (Spearman $r = .31$).

3. Research by Gaesser and Whitbourne (1985) indicates that intrinsic work satisfaction among blue-collar men is positively related to their marital adjustment.

Chapter 8

Earning a Living:
The Impact of Wife's Employment

An excellent Wife, who can find?
For her worth is far above jewels.
She looks for wool and flax,
And works with her hands in delight.
She considers a field and buys it;
From her earnings she plants a vineyard.
She senses that her gain is good;
Her lamp does not go out at night.
She makes linen garments, and sells them,
And supplies belts to the tradesmen.
She looks well to the ways of her household,
And does not eat the bread of idleness.

—Selected verses from Proverbs 31,
New American Standard Bible

In several respects, Bob and Carol Curtis fit the prototype of the yuppy couple. Both are well educated and highly successful professionals; Bob is a department administrator for a social service agency and Carol is a consultant to a prominent advertising firm in Chicago. Both have a strong achievement orientation and both find fulfillment in their respective careers. Neither are particularly religious—at least in the conventional sense.

With two healthy children, a house in a fashionable neighborhood, and money in the bank, it might be said that the Curtises have it made. That's pretty much how they see it. In fact, when asked if he had any particularly worries or concerns, Bob Curtis could think of none. After some thought, all Carol could think of was a crack in the sidewalk outside their house.

In looking back on their seventeen years of marriage, neither Bob nor Carol could recall a time when their lives had not been rushed. It was not that they had planned it this way, or even desired it. On the contrary, the two of them delayed getting married for four years while they completed their college degrees, and then two more years on top of that while Bob worked on a Master's degree before finally getting married. Once married, they put off starting their two-child family for almost three additional years while they struggled to launch their respective careers and save enough for a down payment on a house.

Asked if she had any regrets, Carol said, "I do wish that I had been able to work less when the kids were small. In fact Bob urged me to do so. But there were payments to make on the house and I had just landed some large advertising accounts. I worked hard to get those accounts and I guess there was just no way that I was going to just turn them over to somebody else. It's not that I'm one of those money-grabbing sorts. I really like what I do. I enjoy the challenge of taking a difficult assignment, putting a (advertising) program together and making it work. And I don't think my kids have suffered because of my working, not really. If anything my working has forced them to develop the kind of independence they'll need when they get older."

At the time of our interview, Carol had gone back to school to work on an MBA degree. Since she was still working full-time, Bob took on greater responsibility for child care. Yet both noted that they frequently disagreed about who should do the housework. When asked what would make life easier, Carol said a maid.

Despite their disagreements, Carol and Bob described their marriage as a good one. Both indicated that they are very much in love. Although there was a time when they had considered divorce, both said that if they had it to do over, they would marry the same person again.

The Curtises are one of a growing number of dual-earner couples. Their rate of increase represents one of the most phenomenal changes to occur in our society in recent decades. Wives, of course, have always worked — and often very hard. What has changed is the location of their work (many more wives work outside the home) and their financial remuneration. In 1950, a scant one-fourth of married mothers were employed outside the home. Today the proportion has increased to more than half (U.S. Bureau of the Census, 1984). Christiantown wives conform quite closely to this pattern with 50% holding jobs outside the home.

THE IMPACT OF WIFE-EMPLOYMENT ON THE MARRIAGE RELATIONSHIP

The ever-increasing proportion of married mothers pursuing employment has prompted questions about the impact of this phenomenon on the marriage relationship (Booth, Johnson, & White, 1984). An especially strong negative reaction has come from the pens of some conservative Christian writers. One such writer rests his argument against women working outside the home on what he supposes to be the nature of women and God's intended "order":

> A sign of the moral breakdown of our times is the ease with which husbands visit this responsibility upon their wives. Working wives and working mothers have become so much a part of our culture that we scarcely stop to consider what a departure this is from Divine Order, or the deleterious effect it has upon family life.
>
> The burden of caring for the support of the family lies upon the man. The woman is glad to draw this burden to herself, for her character always tends toward watchfulness in material things. But the burden is too heavy for her. Stronger shoulders are given to the man; he has a greater natural strength of mind to enable him to stand up under the pressure of these cares. The heart of a woman is more easily discouraged and dejected. God has made her that way. Therefore, also, he has spared her the responsibility for supporting the family. (Christenson, 1970, pp. 127-128)

Others, writing to the same audience, feel differently about working wives and maintain that Christians simply have to accept it (Campolo, 1987).

Much of the debate over the impact of wife-employment on the marriage relationship has focused on the fact that nationally the divorce rates for employed women are higher than those for full-time housewives (Nock, 1987). Some have taken this as evidence of the harm that the working wife phenomenon may inflict on a marriage and observe that the problems and stresses often prove too great to handle for many dual-earner couples (Michael, 1977; Schoen & Urton, 1979; Spitz, 1988). But others (Wang & Stellway, 1987, p. 85) have taken issue with the notion that wife-employment and divorce are causally connected. They point out that such employment often gives a woman an added measure of freedom or security that allows her to get out of an already bad marriage. They further observe that the conditions for divorce might well exist before the wife begins to work but that once she is gainfully employed, she feels more capable of surviving on her own without her "breadwinner" husband. They also cite a study by Johnson and Skinner (1986) which found that significant numbers of women obtain work in order to prepare themselves for divorce.

There is evidence of greater communication and higher levels of self-disclosure within dual-earner couples when compared with single-earner couples (Rosenfeld & Welsh, 1985; Simpson & England, 1981). This was certainly true for Bob and Carol Curtis who, we noted, reported a degree of communication and companionship that was well above the average. Suspecting that this might be true for working couples in general, we checked to see whether wives and their husbands report exchanging ideas more frequently than do couples where the wife is not employed. And this is exactly what we found (Figure 8.1).

So far things look pretty good for dual-earner marriages. But what about marital happiness? Do those in employed-wife marriages experience greater marital happiness than those in unemployed-wife marriages? This seems like a logical possibility, particularly since other studies have found a positive correspondence between wife-employment and marital happiness (Caplow et al., 1982, p. 99). Upon comparing the marital happiness ratings of employed wives and their husbands with those for work-at-home wives and their husbands, however, the relationship is less apparent (Figure 8.2). Compared to their counterparts, a slightly higher percent-

FIGURE 8.1. Wife employment and reported "exchange of exciting ideas"

===

Employment Status   Daily exchange of exciting ideas
(number)   (husbands and wives)

Husbands and
Employed Wives   =============================== 42%
(n=50)
Husbands and
Unemployed Wives   ============== 22%
(n=50)

Kruskal-Wallis H = 4.55; p = ≤ .04

FIGURE 8.2. Percent of employed wives and unemployed wives and their husbands who rate their repsective marriages as very happy

```
================================================================

Sex and Employment Status      Percent with Very Happy
       (number)                         Marriages

----------------------------------------------------------------

Employed Wives           =============================== 52%
     (n=25)
Unemployed Wives         ========================================= 69.6%
     (n=23)
Husbands with
Employed Wives           ===================================== 64%
     (n=25)
Husbands with
Unemployed Wives         ========================================= 69.6%
     (n=23)

----------------------------------------------------------------
```

Kruskal-Wallis H. for Employed and Unemployed Wives = 1.31; p = < .10
Kruskal-Wallis H for Husbands of Employed and Unemployed Wives = .36; p < .10

age of full-time housewives and their husbands rate their marriages as very happy. However, in his review of the literature, Drake Smith (1985) found that when several control measures were introduced, no difference in marital adjustment between wife-employment and non-employment was apparent.

In examining our data, we did find two reasons why wives employed outside the home may experience more marital stress than their work-at-home counterparts: these include the way in which roles are allocated in dual-earner marriages and the way the responsibility load is managed.

HOW DO WORKING COUPLES HANDLE THE WORK LOAD

In her study of U.S. women at work, sociologist Linda Waite (1980) found that employed wives put in close to two and one-half hours a day on housework while the contribution of their husbands amounts to less than one-half hour a day. We do not know how household chores are allocated among Christiantowners but we did find that when the wife is employed, couples disagree over household chores more often than when she isn't employed (Figure 8.3). It appears that dual-earner couples, in trying to adjust to a new pattern, may be having difficulty negotiating on who should do what around the house. What makes the situation more difficult is that spouses tend to think that they assume more responsibility for household duties than their partners think they do (Hiller & Philliber, 1986).

WHAT ABOUT CHILD CARE?

We asked our Christiantown couples to indicate the proportion of time that they and their spouses spend in child care. We found that Christiantown husbands are somewhat more inclined to participate in care for their children when their wives do not work, but the degree of role sharing in this area is far from equitable. While 86% of work-at-home wives report that they assume major responsibility for child care, nearly two-thirds (64%) of employed wives continue to assume major responsibility. In this respect Christiantowners

FIGURE 8.3. Employment status of wife and agreement on household chores

==

Employment Status of Wife (number)	Percent of wives and their husbands agreeing on household chores

----

Employed Wives and their husbands (n=50)   ========================== 50%

Unemployed Wives and their husbands (n=50)   ================================== 70%

Kruskal-Wallis H = 3.76; p = .05

seem to reflect the common pattern, where fathers spend comparatively little time caring for children, whether or not the wife is employed (Barnett & Baruch, 1987; Coverman & Sheley, 1986; Miller
& Garrison, 1982).

ARE WORKING WIVES APPRECIATED?

A second situation which may make the marriage relationship
less attractive for employed wives involves the appreciation — or
lack thereof — that employed wives receive from their husbands.
Despite the fact that working women continue to shoulder the major
burden of child care, their husbands give them comparatively little
credit for their efforts. Forty-five percent of husbands with work-at-
home wives rated their wives' parenting as excellent. But only
about half that percentage of husbands with employed wives (24%)
gave their wives' parenting an excellent rating. Barring other responsibility trade-offs of which these investigations are not aware,
working wives seem to be caught in a double bind. They don't
receive sufficient help from their husbands to offset the added
workload, but they are effectively graded down by their husbands in
terms of their parental performance.

The fact that working husbands tend to rate their wives' parenting
less favorably raises a question. Are the children of working parents
indeed worse off when both of their parents work? Although our
study did not focus on this issue specifically, numerous studies have
sought to determine the impact. In reviewing the results of these
numerous studies, Moore, Spain, and Bianchi (1984) and Spitz
(1988) have expressed surprise at how few direct effects on children — of either a positive or negative nature — have been linked to
their mothers' employment.

Another area in which appreciation seems lacking involves the
contribution a working wife makes to the total family income. We
noticed that working women and their husbands differ only slightly
in their rating of the husband's income. (Just under 35% of husbands with employed wives rated their own income as "very adequate"; just over 42% of their wives rated their husbands' income
this way.) But when rating the husband's and wife's combined in-

come, over 61% of employed wives rated it "very adequate," but only 42% of their husbands rated it such.

It appears, then, that dual-earner couples like the Curtises have more difficulty allocating domestic tasks and agree less on the outcome of their negotiations. Husbands are also less inclined to value the contribution their working wives make to the family.

HOW IMPORTANT IS WIVES' WORK SATISFACTION?

In the last chapter we noted how a husband's work satisfaction influenced the marriage relationship. Our data indicate that the same is true for wives. Whereas just over one-third (36%) of wives with low-to-moderate job satisfaction rated their marriages as "very happy," two-thirds of wives with high job satisfaction rated their marriages this way (Figure 8.4). In fact, by controlling for wives' job satisfaction, the marital happiness ratings of satisfied wives and their husbands closely approximate the happiness ratings of unemployed wives and their husbands. Once again, given the size of our sample, the difference in the ratings is not large enough to rule out a chance occurrence. However, Terry and Scott (1987), using a similar-sized sample, also failed to find a significant relationship.) Yet data we obtained from the 1987 General Social Survey reveals much the same relationship between employed wives' work satisfaction and their marital happiness. It is interesting to note that for this national sample, employed wives with high work satisfaction report a higher percentage of very happy marriages than do full-time housewives (Figure 8.5).

Despite the controversy, wife-employment does not appear to have the negative effect on marriage predicted by some. Indeed, there are some positive advantages, such as increased couple communication, which may derive from it. But forging new roles while balancing household and child care responsibilities continue to present a major challenge. Compared to their unemployed counterparts, employed wives tend to be busier, yet are often not as appreciated, particularly as parents. In this next chapter we turn our attention to the parenting experience.

FIGURE 8.4. Marital happiness ratings of husbands and wives according to wives' work satisfaction level

==

Wives' Job   Percent with "Very Happy"
   Satisfaction Level   Marriages

Wives with High
   Satisfaction (n=12)   ==================================. 67%

Husbands of Wives with High
   Satisfaction (n=12)   =================================== 64%

Wives with Low-to-Moderate
   Satisfaction (n=11)   ================== 36%

Husbands of Wives with Low-to-Moderate
   Satisfaction (n=11)   ==================. 45%

Cell frequencies are too small to obtain statistical significance at the .05 level.

FIGURE 8.5. Marital happiness ratings according to employment status of wife and work satisfaction — for white married mothers between 20 and 50 years of age

===

```
Employment Status  &              Percent Rating their
Job Satisfaction                  Marriage "Very Happy"
(number)
```

```
Full-Time
  Housewives          *************************** 58.6%
  (n=116)
Employed Wives/Very
  Satisfied w/ Job    ******************************************* 80%
  (n=44)
Employed Wives/Low to
  Moderately Satisfied ************************** 52.3%
  (n=44)
```

_____

Kruskal-Wallis H for housewives and employed wives with high job satisfaction = 6.05; p = .01
Kruskal-Wallis H for housewives and employed wives with less job satisfaction = .52; p = ≤.10

107

Chapter 9

The Parental Experience

Despite the increasing complexity of the task, parenthood remains the single preserve of the amateur.

—Alvin Toffler, *Future Shock* (1970, pp. 207-208)

Over the space of five short years, Paul and Rachael Anthony's four children were born. Rachael maintains that this is an ideal number. How did she arrive at that conclusion? As she explained it, "My husband and I come from Catholic families. There were six kids in my family. Paul's had four. The fact that we're Catholic dictated that we have four in a row. Oh it was pretty rough when the kids were small," she confided. "Having four preschoolers in the house was exhausting. But Paul and I agreed before we were married that he'd work and I'd stay home and care for the kids." Would she do it again? "Yes," she replied, "though I'd spread them further apart."

Rachael's husband Paul has a somewhat different outlook. Paul described himself as Catholic but, unlike his wife, he admitted to having some doubts about God's existence. Paul said three or four children were an ideal number. But in explaining how he arrived at that number, Paul's reason was more pragmatic than his wife's religious explanation. "I've seen a lot of people with two children," he said. "I don't like two-child families. They're too self-centered." Still, Paul admits that four children are "a weary and awesome responsibility," and added, "they're a crushing burden on their mother when they're young." Then somewhat philosophically

Paul remarked, "One can learn from the adversity of a large family."

At the time of our interview, three of the Anthony's four children were in their teen years. Paul, who puts long hours into his practice as a clinical psychologist, regrets that his work prevents him from spending more time with his children. Rachael commented that compared with the preschool years, having teen-agers has been the most difficult time in their marriage. Rachael also regrets that her husband does not spend more time with their children.

Occasionally one hears of parents who, because of the difficulties and hardships their children have brought them, express regrets about ever having had them. Although these sentiments may be true for some, they hardly describe the Anthony's feelings. Nor do they convey the feelings of most Christiantown parents. On the contrary, one overriding impression from our respondents is that despite the worries and frustrations that come with parenthood, they enjoy being parents. In fact our parents, who had an average of two and three-tenths children, told us that if they had it to do over again they would have the same number. Some added that if time and money had been no obstacle, they would like to have had even more. In only a couple of instances did parents say that they wished they would have had fewer children.

SOURCES OF PARENT SATISFACTION: A TYPOLOGY OF CHILD REARING ORIENTATIONS

To help determine just what Christiantown parents were satisfied about, we asked a randomly selected subset of Christiantowners what they saw as some of the good things about having children. In analyzing the many and varied responses, four broad categories of satisfaction surfaced.

Child-Centered: Satisfaction Through Observation

When recounting the good things about being parents, our respondents often began by remarking how much fun it was to observe their children. They valued their innocence. They were fascinated by their thought processes. They were enamored, even transfixed, at the sight of their offspring growing and developing before their eyes. As one mother of two explained, "It's such a joy to see them grow and develop; just watching them learn and grow mentally, socially, and emotionally—it's fascinating." Another mother celebrated what she termed, "the wonder of watching their little thought processes develop."

These child-centered sources of satisfaction were mentioned by most parents, but other sources emerged as well.

Relationship-Centered: Satisfaction Through Interaction

A few parents reflected on the husband-wife relationship and how children had strengthened or improved it. One parent remarked on the beauty of the child-grandparent relationship. But the relationship mentioned most often was that between parent and child. "They triple love," said one mother of five, "giving and caring are practiced more."

For many parents, children provide a highly valued source of companionship. As one father of six put it, "With children you have someone to do something with; there's never a dull moment; the house is more lively with the kids around."

Self-Centered:
Satisfaction Through Personal Growth and Fulfillment

Several kinds of growth emerged in this more complex category. One type involved the contribution children make to their parents' development; some parents believe that children afford them the capacity to see things from a child's point of view, thereby increasing their understanding of children and the world. Others echoed Paul Anthony's conviction that children build character traits such as patience, tolerance, thoughtfulness, generosity, self-understanding, and social adjustment. One mother summarized it well: "Children contribute to becoming a whole person."

A second type of self-centered motive concerned need fulfillment. The comments of a number of parents suggested the important role children play in fulfilling their parents' need to nurture. "It may sound funny," said one father," but it feels good having someone depend on you so." Another father expressed special delight in being able to show his children "everything that's around them." Mothers in particular were inclined to indicate that children met an emotional need. "It (motherhood) just completely fulfilled me," said one mother. "The children give my life meaning and purpose."

Vicarious pleasure constituted a third type of self-centered parenting. In the words of a Christiantown mother, "Being a parent is a way of renewing your own childhood." Although such vicarious satisfaction tends to be a passive experience, it does not have to be. One father of two sons maintained that his children permitted him to get out and do things he enjoyed doing as a kid. "I'd look pretty silly racing down a hill on a toboggan by myself," he said, "but I can get away with it when my kids are along."

Still a fourth type of self-centered parental satisfaction is ego-enhancement. In some societies this motive is expected and accepted, but in a society that stresses the integrity of each individual, it is often feared that using a child to enhance a parent's ego amounts to putting the parent's welfare ahead of the child's. Love is supposed to define the parent-child relationship. And love, as psychologist Harry Overstreet reminds us, "implies not the possession of that person, but the affirmation of that person. It means granting him, gladly, the full right to his humanhood" (1949, p. 153).

Since we believed this to be a widely accepted conviction, we did not expect that parents would readily admit to using their children for their own ego enhancement. Yet this motive was clearly evident in the remarks of some. The most conspicuous reference was contained in a comment by a father of an only child. "Kids give you an ego trip," he told us. "It gives you a lot of pride in yourself when you can see them follow your instruction." The comments of other parents, however, were a bit more subtle. After explaining how much he and his wife liked music, one father of three recalled the delight that he and his wife took in seeing their children develop their musical talents and share them with others. "It gives me such a thrill," he said, "to see the kids perform at school and in church musicals."

Transcendent: Beyond Self and Family

At a time when the two-child family is fast becoming the ideal, those who opt for large families are often regarded as deviant. Some time ago one of our students came under attack from others in her class when she expressed her desire for four or five kids. In defense of her position, she quipped, "My children will help make this world a better place in which to live." Few Christiantown parents articulated this idea so strongly. Yet the comments of some might be construed to suggest this idea. One mother of three, for example, defended parenthood as "a chance to raise someone else to take your place in the world."

When transcendent sources of satisfaction were expressed, they often contained a distinctly religious theme. One father of six told us, for example, that "children are a gift from the Lord, a privilege entrusted to us." We shall give more attention to this topic in the last section as we consider the impact of religion on procreation and socialization.

PROBLEMS OF PARENTHOOD: THE OTHER SIDE OF THE COIN

In their book, *Parents in Contemporary America*, E. E. LeMasters and John DeFrain (1983) comment that many prospective parents are misled by a prevailing myth of parenthood which emphasizes the joys and benefits of having children while virtually ignoring the disadvantages. It was evident from the remarks of some Christiantowners that they had had in fact very naive notions concerning the requirements of parenthood. As one mother of three expressed it, "I thought you just played with them, fed them, and put them to sleep. Boy, was I in for a surprise."

From a "functional" standpoint such naiveté may actually be beneficial. If people were fully briefed about the negative side of parenting, they might not be so willing to take on the job and society might not succeed in replacing itself. To help clarify the actual situation, we asked our Christiantown informants to comment on the difficulties they encountered as parents. It did not take much effort for them to recount a number of initial as well as continuing adjustment problems.

Initial Adjustment Problems

Many Christiantown parents experienced adjustment problems just after the birth of their children. This became quite apparent when they commented on what they considered to be the most difficult time of their marriage. Most recalled a time when their children were quite young. Dave Jacobson's experience illustrates the situation well:

> Margaret and I were in our ninth year of marriage when the twins were born. We had waited a long time for this event and were, needless to say, quite thrilled. But then we began to feel really confined. We had anticipated the added expense of having a baby and had put some money aside. Naturally we didn't expect to have twins and this has resulted in some added pressure. But the hardest part was adjusting to the tremendous demand that they made on our time. Somehow we just weren't as prepared as we thought we'd be.

Studies vary in their description of parenthood as a "crisis" experience (Belsky, 1985; Gilbert, 1982). What some studies fail to consider is that parents sometimes find themselves going through several adjustments simultaneously. One mother told us about the stress she experienced when both of her parents died the same year their first child was born. It is not hard to understand the grave effects of such a catastrophe. Yet for some people, giving up a meaningful role because of parenthood can be almost as traumatic. Mary Newmeyer knows about such trauma. After her first child was born, Mary left a nursing career which had given her recognition, fulfillment, and a measure of independence. Although she had been convinced that motherhood would be just as meaningful, the pleasure was a different kind. Now, five years after the birth of her second child, Mary is beginning to think seriously about resuming her nursing career.

If adjustment were merely a problem of accommodating to a first time experience, it would seem that adjustment to subsequent births would be easier. Yet parents often singled out the birth of their second or third child as the most difficult time in their marriage. These responses were particularly common when parents had their children close together. For John Breward the most difficult period came shortly after his discharge from military duty. "We had several kids in diapers all at once," he recalled. "What made it worse was that we lost a lot of friends we had while I was in the service. I remember feeling deserted and very much alone."

Close spacing, what sociologists call "child density," also proved a problem for Mary Schuler. Mary, a mother of six, recalled, "In the early part of our marriage we had lots of children. It was quite a responsibility, as you can imagine. We were having babies so often. And in those days we didn't know how to prevent them. There was no birth control except what was traditional." Like Rachael Anthony, Mrs. Schuler told us that if she had it to do over again she would have the same number but be sure to spread them further apart.

Who Has to Adjust to Parenthood More?

Economists indicate that the period of family expansion, when children are being added to the family, is frequently a time of financial strain. During this period a husband may come under particular pressure as increasing expenses threaten to exceed his earning capacities. Of course, financial concerns are not borne exclusively by the husband. Yet it is still the husband who internalizes the traditional cultural expectation that he is responsible for meeting the family's financial needs (Weiss, 1985). Because of a husband's "male socialization," we might anticipate that parenthood is particularly stressful for Christiantown husbands.

But traditional expectations continue to affect the wife as well (Weitzman, 1985). In her mother role she is supposed to be a full-time parent. According to the traditional standard, she rightfully spends most of her day with her preschool children — feeding them, clothing them, nursing them when they are ill, and responding to their many other continuous needs. Since this responsibility often cuts into her other activities, the wife, like her husband, may find that parenthood is a difficult adjustment.

Defenders of the traditional pattern point out that it is appropriately complementary. They explain that one person must necessarily assume primary responsibility for securing needed funds and the best person for that job is the husband. Similarly, another person must assume primary responsibility for child care and the fittest person for that job is the wife. Yet many modern couples have become discontented with the concept of complementary parenting. In the name of companionship they are attempting to implement a new approach: shared parenting. Consistent with this approach, fathers are sharing more child care responsibilities such as feedings and diaper changes — activities traditionally performed by the mother — without fear of compromising their masculinity. Wives also have begun to share with their husbands the burden of meeting their family's financial needs.

To obtain an indication of parental adjustment experience, we asked our Christiantown couples, "Who do you think has to adjust to parenthood more: the husband, the wife, or both about the same?" If couples are truly sharing the responsibilities of parenthood, they should indicate similar adjustment. Yet less than 30% of the parents we interviewed indicated that both have to adjust to parenthood to the same degree. Christiantowners designated the wife over the husband three to one as the person having to make the greater adjustment. Husbands tended to be in agreement with their wives on this point. There is evidence to indicate that Christiantown parents are far from unique in this regard (Harriman, 1983). These findings suggest that the personal and marital changes which accompany parenthood are inclined to make the transition a particularly difficult one for mothers.

Given the difficulties that parents often encounter with young children, we were curious to know what they do to adjust. Few parents had a ready reply to this question. Most noted, however, that their adjustment improved as their children grew older. To verify this, we asked parents to recall how satisfied they had been at various times in their marriage. As is evident in Figure 9.1, less than half the parents indicated high satisfaction levels before their

FIGURE 9.1.* Satisfaction levels at selected stages of life

```
=================================================================

Stage of Life          Percent expressing high satisfaction
    (n=48)                              (**)


Before Children
   Arrived            ***********48%***********


First Years with
   Infant             **********44%**********


Preschool Children
   At Home            *********38%*********


All Children
   At School          ****************65%****************.

-----------------------------------------------------------------
Kruskal-Wallis H (satisfaction dependent) = 7.69; p = .05.
*Note: The same set of parents rated each stage of the life cycle.
```

116

children started school. Only after their children reached school age did the majority of parents register high satisfaction. By this time most children have passed through diapers, the "terrible twos," and they have become less dependent in many ways. But more important, school now occupies significant portions of the child's time. The impact of school, it turns out, extends far beyond the education of youngsters since it has a significant impact on the life satisfaction and marital adjustment of parents.

Continuing Adjustment Problems

In probing problem areas, we posed several kinds of questions to our respondents. "What things tend to worry or concern you the most?" "What, if anything, would you like to see changed in your marriage?" "What, if anything, would help make your family life easier?" Again and again parents expressed concerns over lack of time.

Looking for circumstances which give rise to such concerns, we checked to see whether the wife was employed. We were surprised to find that this factor made no appreciable difference. What did become apparent, though, was a link between lack of time and family size. One-fourth of parents with one or two children, but nearly two-thirds (65%) of parents with three or four children, mentioned time as a major concern.

In light of the demands that children place on their parents, this finding makes sense—except for one thing. Although the majority of parents with three or four children mentioned the lack of time as a problem, less than one-fifth of those with five or six children made mention of it. Why this inconsistency? Why should parents with large numbers of children make some reference to a shortage of time less often than families with one or two children?

Hint of a plausible answer to this question came from Mary Schuler, a mother of six. She told us that one of the good things about having children is that they are a lot of help around the house. Her comment suggests a difference in the way large families are organized. It is logical that three or four children will place more demands on parents' time and energy than will one or two children. But it is inconceivable that parents, regardless of how hard they work, can stretch themselves to meet the demands of five or six children without "exhausting" themselves. For the sake of survival, then, families must undergo some fundamental reorganization as they become larger. This very likely involves a shifting of some parental responsibilities to children.

Our interview responses revealed a number of additional concerns:

1. *Responsibility load*. Parents mentioned taxed energy levels, weariness, and cramped lifestyles such as travel limitations.
2. *Parental role performance*. Several parents articulated anxiety about their parental performance. Anxieties arose over the handling of parent-child conflicts, school problems, problems "fitting in," etc., as well as concern about being a good counselor and role model. Parents often expressed belief that their children would turn out all right if they applied the proper skills.
3. *Special situations*. Some parents found sickness, sleeplessness, and crowded living conditions especially hard to cope with.
4. *Sibling relationships*. Reference was made to bickering, fighting, and sibling rivalry. (Parents with a single child were spared this problem.)
5. *Finances*. Several parents are worried about adequately providing for their children's financial needs. (What is considered "adequate provision" obviously varies with social class and peer comparison.)
6. *Personal property*. Concern about protecting personal property from waste or destruction by children is not only a concern of parents of young children but a concern of parents of teen-agers as well.
7. *Social environment*. Some parents are concerned over the direction of the society, the economy, or the world at large. Others were concerned about how this environment will affect how their children turn out.

Just how do parents want their children to turn out? To get an idea, we asked them about their parenting goals.

MAJOR PARENTING GOALS

> What do I want my children to learn by the time they leave home? I want them to learn that they can get almost anything they want through hard work. —*Henry Hodges, company executive*

> I want my children to be able to look a person—any person— right in the eye and say "hello." —*Carl Williams, media technician*

Goal statements such as these give insight into the content of the parents' own values. Henry Hodges' goal statement, for example, reveals a strong concern for self-sufficiency. Carl Williams' comment reveals a high regard for self-acceptance. These values reflect concerns that have been instilled in people by their own parents while growing up. They also reflect lessons extracted from their adulthood experience. In examining parents' responses to our question about their parenting goals, we found numerous references to how a child will relate to himself/herself and to how he/she will relate to others.

Relationship to Self

Carl Williams' valuing self-acceptance indicates one kind of healthy relationship to self. Concerns for personal happiness, self-respect, self-fulfillment, and psychological adjustment are other essential ways of relating to oneself. About a fourth of the parents we interviewed referred to these child-rearing goals.

Responsibility to Others

A slightly larger proportion of parents expressed a desire that their children become sensitive to other people's needs and responsible for their welfare. Characteristics such as empathy, understanding, love, dependability, and trustworthiness were mentioned frequently.

Do Christiantown parents balance their emphasis on children's responsibility to themselves with an emphasis on their responsibility to others? Comments from a few parents reveal a concern for both. For example, one mother said that she wanted her children to be wise enough to avoid being taken advantage of, but also was concerned that they not take advantage of others. However, most parents tended to restrict their comments to just one of the two relationship areas.

Considering that children are inclined to focus on their own well-being without much instruction, it could be argued that Christiantown parents ought to give more emphasis to developing in their children a healthy regard for others. Some parents placed a high priority on this value, but many either did not mention it or mentioned it only indirectly.

Robert Bellah and other social critics view this situation with concern. In their best-selling book, *Habits of the Heart*, Bellah and his associates (Bellah, Madsen, Sullivan, Swindler, & Tipton, 1985, pgs. 142-166) point out that while self-actualization and personal fulfillment may be justified, when they become the exclusive aim of child rearing, children may fail to develop the kind of commitment required for responsible marital and parental role performance. What is needed, the authors maintain, is a balanced emphasis on responsibility to self and regard for others. We shall examine this issue further as we consider the impact of religion on parenting goals.

THE IMPACT OF RELIGION

Procreation

As we alluded to in Chapter 4, one of the more dramatic ways in which religion registers an impact on marriage is through the influence it has on family size. The impact of religion was certainly evident in Rachael Anthony's case. And it is apparent from Figure 9.2 that more conservative believers are indeed inclined to have larger families than those with less conservative beliefs. Nor is this relationship unique to Christiantowners. Other studies, including our analysis of data from the 1987 General Social Survey (Appendix A, Table A.6), have uncovered a similar relationship. (Scanzoni & Scanzoni, 1981, pp. 513-516; Zopf, 1984, pp. 15-16; 41-42.)

FIGURE 9.2. How religious belief corresponds to fertility

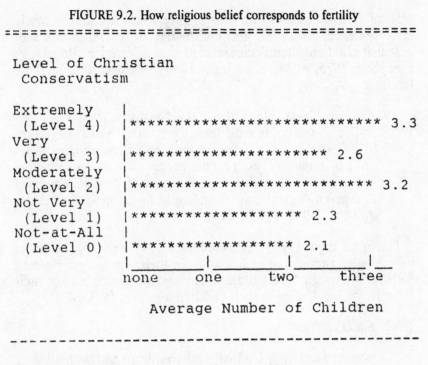

```
Level of Christian
Conservatism

Extremely   |
  (Level 4) |****************************** 3.3
Very        |
  (Level 3) |********************** 2.6
Moderately  |
  (Level 2) |***************************** 3.2
Not Very    |
  (Level 1) |****************** 2.3
Not-at-All  |
  (Level 0) |**************** 2.1
            |_____|_____|_____|__
            none     one      two     three

        Average Number of Children
```

Spearman Rank Order Correlation = .39; p = ≤.001

In their zeal to promote parenthood, some Christian writers have appealed to "human nature" and to a once-popular "instinct psychology." The following quote from a popular Christian writer illustrates this attitude:

> Children fulfill the psychic design of your mind. Man's mind has to be severely warped to feel "unnatural'" about fatherhood or motherhood. God has given certain commands — and these produce that "natural" feeling essential to a happy life. Parenthood is such an instinct. (LaHaye & LaHaye, 1976, p. 185)

We have already noted how children frequently provide their parents with a feeling of satisfaction and fulfillment. But the argument that children are essential for a happy life seems to lack validity in the experience of many. In fact the findings of several studies suggest that children often decrease happiness (Converse, Rogers, & Campbell, 1975, p. 38). Sociologist Henry Holstege sums up these findings:

> There is considerable evidence that for many, if not most parents, child-rearing is a difficult, frustrating, and anxiety-producing process. . . . Couples with no children indicate, on public opinion surveys, a higher degree of marital satisfaction than couples with children. A majority of American women have psychological trauma in adjusting to their first child. (Holstege, 1982, pp. 20-21)

Perhaps a major key to understanding why conservative believers have greater numbers of children lies in their hope of propagating their faith through their children. This would be one part of their concern for inculcating in their children a respect for God.

Child Socialization

> Love the Lord your God with all your heart and with all your soul and with all your strength. These commandments that I give you today are to be upon your hearts. Impress them upon your children. Talk about them when you sit at home. . . . (Deuteronomy 6:5-7, New International Version)

The remarks of many Christiantown parents reveal a vital concern that their children develop a close relationship with God. The following statements are exemplary: "I want my children to learn to love God and to place Him first in their lives"; "I want my children to have a close, growing relationship with God"; "I want them to be willing to do things God's way;" "I want my children to trust in Christ as savior." As one father put it, "I want my children to learn that the life that satisfies lies in doing God's will."

The frequency with which parents made such statements was closely paralleled by their religious beliefs. Indeed, the number of parents who expressed a concern that their children develop a "trusting" and "obedient" relationship with God (about one-third of those who were asked about child-rearing goals) increased dramatically with increased levels of conservatism. (Figure 9.3) It is quite apparent that the conservative believers of Christiantown are vitally concerned with passing their own religious values onto their children.

In considering the implications of this concern it may be helpful to recall our earlier discussion regarding the need for a balance between parental emphasis on responsibility to self and on responsibility to others. How does parental concern for developing a "right" relationship with God affect this balance? When it comes to specific cases, it is hard to say for sure. Two-thirds of parents who mentioned religious concerns mentioned other goals as well and were about evenly divided in their mention of goals emphasizing self-relationships and other-relationships. However, implicit in the remarks of some parents was the idea that a proper relationship to God must, of necessity, include a proper relationship with oneself and with one's fellow man. When asked what he most wanted for his three children, one father put it this way: "To love God and to follow in His way. This means to be patient and responsible, to respect the rights of others, to make the world a better place in which to live."

Given the many pressures confronting today's parents, the fact that Christiantowners enjoyed being parents is reassuring. But it is evident from the experience of Christiantowners — and others — that prospective parents need to bear in mind that the child rearing years, particularly the preschool years, can be difficult indeed. Growing families frequently experience financial pressures as husbands, who are often the primary income earners, struggle to establish themselves in a job or profession. Meanwhile their wives end up shouldering the major burden of child care.

Parenting requires a continual process of reorientation to the child at each age and to the parent-child relationship as both grow older. An examination of parental attitudes and ultimate child-rearing goals must necessarily be a part of this process. But parents must also reorient themselves to one another since the nature of their parenting experience changes as their children move through the stages of development.

In the next chapter we shall consider the lessons that Christiantowners have derived from their varied experiences.

FIGURE 9.3. How religious beliefs correspond to parents' concern that their children develop a right relationship with God

==

Level of Christian
Conservatism

```
Extremely     |************************************************.
(level 4;n=15)|
Very          |**********36%*****
(level 3;n=14)|
Moderately    |*13%*.
(level 2;n=9) |
Not Very      |0%
(level 1;n=3) |
Not-at-All    |0%
(level 0;n=7) |___|___|___|___|___|___|___|___|___|___|
              10%  20% 30% 40% 50% 60% 70% 80% 90% 100%
```

[**] Percentage expressing concern that their children develop a
     right relationship with God.

- -

Kruskal-Wallis H (relationship with God dependent) = 26.7; p ≤ .01

Chapter 10

Lessons from Experience:
What They Would Do Different

Marriage is the alarm clock that wakes up the dreamy amour.

—Saffian, *An Irreverent Dictionary of Love and Marriage*
(1966, p. 84)

Reflecting on her sixteen-year marriage, Leanne Monroe says she has learned some hard lessons. As Leanne shared what she had learned, there was a note of bitterness in her voice. "When I married Kirk I suppose I was more concerned about pleasing my folks—finding a husband they'd like—than I was about pleasing myself. But I was very naive. I had a rather glorified concept of marriage. I've since learned that marriage isn't the bed of roses that some people make it out to be. It takes a lot of work and a lot of adjusting. I didn't begin to foresee the many difficulties our different backgrounds would pose. Kirk's background just didn't prepare him to become a parent." When asked what, if anything, she would like to see changed in her marriage, Leanne said that she wished that she and her husband's interests were more compatible. "Why, I'd just like to be able to play a game of tennis with him." What things worry or concern her the most? "I just don't want to see my own mistakes repeated in my children." On the marriage adjustment form we asked her to complete, Leanne indicated that she was not happily married and that she'd have some reservations about marrying the same person again.

When we talked with Leanne's husband, Kirk, we learned that he had a very lonely childhood. Revealingly, Kirk indicated that friendship and companionship were the most satisfying aspects of his marriage. But Kirk also has some regrets. "I wish that I had actualized my parenting potential," he said. "And I wish I had more zest, more ambition. When I come before God, I just hope He'll say, 'well done.'" Asked what he saw as the key to marital success, Kirk said, "You have to realize that you must give more than you get."

Some of the problems that the Monroes are facing in their marriage could not have been foreseen. Within one year of her birth, the couple's first child, Nancy, contracted a degenerative disease. And Kirk himself has not been very healthy. But despite the difficulties that these conditions have caused, Kirk is generally pleased with his family life. When rating his love for his wife and his wife's love for him (on a scale from one to ten), Kirk gave himself an eight and his wife a ten. (His wife Leanne gave both her and her husband a six.) He has no doubt that if he had it to do over, he would marry his wife again.

One of the blessings that time bestows on us is greater wisdom. After being buffeted by experience, we often can anticipate the challenges many young families will encounter, and empathize with their difficulties. We sought to take advantage of the Christiantowners perspective by inquiring about their past problems and regrets, the lessons learned, and the truths they had distilled concerning the ingredients of a successful marriage. This chapter is a report on their collective experience.

CHRISTIANTOWNER COURTSHIP AND MATE SELECTION

The prevailing model of mate selection in America is a process of surveying the field of eligibles, exploring relationships with a few, and then finally narrowing the selection to one person in particular. During the courtship period, people are supposed to collect and process all relevant information bearing on the prospective marriage partner (Murstein, 1970; Stinnett, Walters, & Kaye, 1984, chapter 2).

As the process has evolved, so have certain rules of the game. One of these rules is noninterference by parents and other close relatives. The grave consequences which result from failure to respect this rule were evident in some comments Leanne Monroe made during her interview. She spoke of the great resentment she harbored toward her parents for forcing her to break off with certain men of which they disapproved. In justifying her feelings, she pointed out that she, not her parents, was the one who must live with the decision.

The American courtship system is not without its critics (Balswick & Peek, 1977; Mace & Mace, 1960; Yelsma & Athappilly, 1988). Many maintain that most American courtship is too superficial to provide an adequate basis for what is expected to be a lifetime arrangement. They defend the major role that parents and elders play in mate selection on the grounds that their maturity of experience puts them in a better position to choose and to determine which considerations are most germane to a lasting relationship.

Other critics are concerned over what they see as the competitiveness of the mate selection process (Becker, 1973; Richman, 1977). They note that in North America and Europe, people are forced to compete in courtship much like in a business. In effect, they are pressured to package and market themselves as best they can to insure a favorable rate of exchange. As someone once put it, "courtship is the period during which people are deciding whether they can get someone better." Such phrases as "you have to put your best foot forward" and, "you'd have a real prize if you could land that one," belie the competitiveness of the courtship process.

Such criticisms of American courtship may seem excessive, particularly to those of us who have grown accustomed to it. Yet some of the comments of Christiantowners suggest that there may be reason for concern. When we asked Christiantowners what, if anything, they would have done differently if they had their courtship to do over, one man expressed regret that he had not waited for his parents' approval. Not only did he come to appreciate the wisdom of their input, in time he also realized that the implications of his choice of a mate extended beyond just him and his spouse.

How well do couples manage to penetrate the veneer of superficiality, which critics allege shrouds the courtship process, and really get to know one another? To assess this we inquired to what extent Christiantowners thought they knew their spouses' faults and weaknesses before marriage (Figure 10.1). As it turned out, only three

FIGURE 10.1. How well did Christiantowners know their spouses' faults and weak points before marriage?

Degree of Knowledge	Percentage
"Considerably" or "Very Much" (n=28)	28.6%
"Somewhat" (n=41)	41.8%
"A Little" or "Not At All" (n=29)	29.6%
	total = 100.0%

out of ten indicated that they were very familiar with these before they married.

Does Length of Courtship Make a Difference?

Among those who commented on the length of courtship, only one wished that her courtship had been shorter. (She explained that she had let herself be strung along by her present husband for several years without having much idea where the relationship was going.) But a number of others wished that their courtship had been longer, with one person admitting that she had been too sensitive to peer pressure to get married quickly.

It has often been observed that the longer a couple are acquainted with each other before marriage, the more likely their marriage will be happy and well-adjusted (Stinnett, Walters, & Kaye, 1984, p. 73; Kirkpatrick, 1963). Yet in our sample of Christiantowners we found little evidence of a correspondence between the length of time that our respondents knew their spouses before marriage and their level of marital happiness or adjustment. Wesley Burr (1976, p. 187) notes that studies which have found such a correspondence have not been clear on why it exists. The critical factor may well have less to do with the length of acquaintance per se, and more the extent to which couples spend their time together in ways that contribute to their gaining a realistic knowledge of each other. The comments of several respondents appear to reinforce this point. One husband noted that he had been working too hard in school during his courtship to really get to know his future wife. Another woman complained that the climate of the Christian college campus on which she and her husband did their courting was too artificial. Apparently campus rules were such that she and her fiance found it difficult to spend time together in any intimate context.

A student survey the author conducted at a Christiantown college campus (Wheaton College) suggests that the real problem may be due as much to the rules people associate with the courtship system itself as to any set of campus rules. Inquiring about student attitudes toward what they did on dates, a gap emerged between the things they liked to do and the things they ended up doing. This was particularly a problem for girls who ended up attending more sporting events than they desired. (Interestingly, many of these women preferred participating in sports with their dating partner to merely watching athletes perform.) One rule of dating which these students took seriously required that the man ask the woman for a date — not the other way around — and that a "trustworthy" man have a specific activity in mind when he asks. Women admitted to wishing that things were different, but each felt powerless to change the system. "What would people think?" was a common response (Dating Survey, 1976).

How Important Is it to Know a Spouse's Shortcomings?

Romantic images of the alluring tall, dark, and handsome stranger or the cute, sexy blond do little to convey the importance of knowing much about a person before one falls in love and allegedly looses a measure of objectivity. In fact the experience of romance at times occurs in inverse proportion to any realistic knowledge of the love object (Knox, 1985, p. 230). It is almost as if people fear that the romantic bubble will burst if they get too close to inspect the object of their affection. But our data suggest that those who would substitute romance for a realistic knowledge of a future spouse may be headed for problems. As is evident from Figure 10.2, the chances of Christiantowners having a very happy marriage are substantially reduced when the knowledge of their spouses' weak points and shortcomings is lacking before marriage.

MISCONCEPTIONS OF MARRIAGE

The process by which people learn the attitudes and behaviors which prepare them for the next stage of the life cycle — in this case, marriage — is referred to by sociologists as anticipatory socialization. To the extent that people correctly anticipate the demands of marriage and parenthood, the process is said to be on target (Bell, 1983, pp. 206-218; Komarovsky, 1976, pp. 129-143).

To get an idea how on target the anticipatory socialization of Christiantowners had been, i.e., how accurate their expectations of marriage were, we asked approximately half of our sample participants, "What, if anything, do you know now that you wish you had

FIGURE 10.2. How knowledge of spouse's shortcomings and weak points before marriage relates to marital happiness later on

```
===========================================================
Level of Knowledge       Percent of "Very Happy" Marriages
-----------------------------------------------------------

Little     ************************************. 59%

Some       ***************************************** 66%

Much       ******************************************************* 86%

-----------------------------------------------------------
```

Rank Order Correlation between knowledge of spouse's shortcomings and marital happiness rating = .29; p = ⩽ .01

known before marriage?" It was evident from their remarks that their anticipatory socialization had missed the mark in a number of respects described below.

1. *Ignorance about the difficulty of establishing a marriage relationship.* One husband admitted to being befuddled at discovering that marriage involved much more than having a room mate. Another husband expressed dismay at how much time it takes to communicate (with his wife). Still another reflected on his failure to appreciate that "marriage had to be a cooperative situation." In her attempt to resolve some early issues in her marriage, one woman commented on her discovery of how selfish people can be in seeking their own ways.

2. *Ignorance about the need for new priorities.* "The most difficult thing for me to accept," said one husband and father of two, "was that other things, like my car, my club, and my friends, had to go." Another husband's priorities were shifted when he came to realize that, "some issues, like money, are just not that significant."

3. *Ignorance about the labor involved.* Women were particularly inclined to comment on the work involved in being a housewife and mother. As one woman put it, "I simply didn't realize how much time is taken up with things like housework." Other wives commented "how hard it was to raise children" and "how demanding a family can be — and usually is."

Women were not the only ones to mention the work load. One father of three with a graduate degree and seventeen years of marriage to his credit, commented, "It's a twenty-four-hour a day job you *really have to work at.*" As if to continue the same theme, one housewife noted, "Marriage isn't all romance, it's work. You get out of it what you put into it." Another wife and mother of two reflected the same theme: "It's harder than you hear it is; it is work besides fun."

HOW HARMFUL ARE MISCONCEPTIONS OF MARRIAGE?

These sorts of comments clearly indicate that the expectations that Christiantowners took with them into marriage did not adequately prepare them for the reality to come. But some sociologists have actually suggested that such romantic expectations may function for social continuity. They reason that if people correctly anticipated all of the difficulties that building a viable marriage and raising a family involve, they would not be motivated to take on such a responsibility (Goode, 1982, p. 54; Rubin, 1973). Romantic impressions that convey the joy, excitement, and fun of marriage and family life and romantic stories culminating in "happily ever after" motivate people to move into marriage.

Critics of this so-called functionalist argument point out that this myth of romance often backfires, culminating in frustration, maladjustment, and disgust (Brain, 1976, p. 245). Leanne Monroe, who complained that "marriage isn't a bed of roses," expressed a certain amount of indignation at being misled into thinking it was. Critics point out that many of the factors which once operated to keep people committed to their marital and parental role obligations no longer exist and warn that in their absence, the experience of disillusionment now contributes to desertion and divorce.

Although there are shortcomings in the anticipatory socialization process, the worst fears of the critics do not seem to be realized, at least not for the Christiantowners we interviewed. Despite the problems they encountered, and are still encountering, the majority of Christiantowners find their marriage and family experience quite satisfying. One woman summed up their sentiments: "I was shocked by the cost and effort involved in keeping a house and raising children. But I wouldn't change my decision for a moment."

THE EARLY YEARS OF MARRIAGE: WHAT THEY WOULD DO DIFFERENT

When commenting on the most difficult time in their marriages, more of our respondents mentioned problems encountered in their early years of marriage than those from any other time period. In this respect, Christiantowners are probably not unlike most couples. The fact that most divorces in the U.S. occur in the first three years of marriage says volumes about the adjustment difficulties facing couples during these years (Eshelman, 1985).

What did Christiantowners learn from having gone through the trials of the early marriage years? To answer this question, we asked a subsample of our respondents what they would have done differently. Their responses are instructive.

1. *More patience and respect.* Comments made by a number of husbands indicated that they regretted their own lack of patience and concern for the welfare of their wives and children. Speaking of his wife, one husband said that if he were able to live the early years of his marriage over, "I would have treated her with more respect; been more affectionate toward her. I wasn't always a gentleman." Another father said, "I wish I had been more patient with my kids; I shouldn't have allowed them to upset me so easily."

2. *More communication and self-disclosure.* In his classic book, *The Art of Loving,* Eric Fromm (1956, pp. 29-32) points out that an important but often neglected dimension of love is knowledge of the loved one. How can one really care for another and respond to his/her needs unless the would-be lover knows and understands the object of his affection? It was clear in Fromm's mind that the "art of loving" requires understanding.

One husband we interviewed echoed Fromm's sentiments rather well. Reflecting on what he'd do differently, he said, "I would have gotten to know my wife better; been more aware of her thoughts and feelings. I guess I was more interested in how I felt than how she did."

Knowledge not only requires a readiness to listen to one's spouse, it also requires a willingness to self-disclose. And self-disclosure, if not too one-sided, is conducive to marital satisfaction (Boland & Follingstad, 1987; Hansen & Schuldt, 1984). Yet self-disclosure can be a frightening prospect. As one wife expressed it: "I wish I would have communicated more openly with my husband, but I had such fear of rejection."

For communication to occur at the deepest level, husbands and wives must demonstrate to their mates that they can be trusted to treat what the other reveals with due respect. Such trust takes time to develop. And in the heat of an argument, it is often tempting to turn entrusted information against the discloser. Once that occurs, the re-establishment of trust sufficient for deep self-disclosure will not be easy.

3. *More confrontation of issues*. In their study of conflict coping strategies, Cutler and Dyer (1971) found that it is common for young couples to simply remain quiet and adapt a wait-and-see response in hopes that things will eventually improve. But the investigators point out that this strategy often becomes a substitute for facing the issue directly.

One woman related a particularly stressful time that she and her husband experienced. Right after their marriage, they had taken a particularly difficult missionary assignment in South America. "At the time, it seemed easier to simply ignore the problems we were facing," she said, "but if I had it to do over, I would work through the difficulties—even getting help from a counselor—rather than trying to ignore them."

4. *More time with spouse and children*. The most frequent response to the question of what the respondents would do differently involved regret at not having spent more time with their spouses and children. At times the problem appears to be the result of a quest for career success. After expressing regret over having invested so much of himself in his work, one husband added, "I guess I was just too concerned with trying to achieve some rather unrealistic goals." Husbands were generally the ones to make reference to such regrets, but not always. One woman commented on how she became involved in pursuing a Master's degree when her two children were young and added that if she had it to do over, she would at least wait until her children were in school.

Christiantowners, like many other Americans, attribute their inability to spend sufficient amounts of time with their families to external demands. One woman related how she had to work full-time to pay off sizable medical bills. She wished that she could have worked part-time while her kids were small, but she could not find part-time employment paying enough to cover her financial obligations. Another woman commented on the strain her marriage underwent when her husband was drafted into the armed forces. "The children and I saw very little of him during those years. In fact I was afraid that our children wouldn't know what a father was."

Other Christiantowners experienced time pressures and strained relationships because they chose to pursue nonmaterial ideals. The couple who took on a mission assignment in South America serves as one example. The husband who gave up a good-paying job in industry to return to school to prepare for "the ministry" is another. His family had to substantially alter their material lifestyle as a consequence of this decision.

For many Christiantowners, lack of time has proven to be a chronic problem. When asked what they would most like to see changed in their marriages, a number said that they would like to be able to spend more time together as a couple and as a family.

WHAT CHRISTIANTOWNERS SEE AS THE KEY TO MARITAL SUCCESS

Taken together, our sample of Christiantowners have accumulated an impressive total of 1,498 years of marriage experience. We endeavored to tap some of the wisdom they had accumulated during their years of marriage by asking a subsample of Christiantowners (forty-eight in all) to comment on what they believed to be the key to marital success. Their terminology varied, but the most frequently given advice is contained in the categories that follow. The ordering of the categories reflects the frequency with which their content was mentioned.

1. *Communicate regularly and communicate openly.* The most frequently noted key to marital success was communication. Christiantowners were concerned that couples keep one another informed about events of the day and in their lives, as well as what they think of these events and how they react to them. Stress was placed on the need to share feelings. Several respondents emphasized that communication needs to be a two-way effort. Indeed, researchers are learning that two-way sharing is essential if in-depth self-disclosure is to occur (Johnson, 1973).

A marriage counselor once related a humorous account of one-sided communication. It seems that one of his clients complained to him that she and her husband did not communicate. After some discussion, the couple agreed to set aside fifteen minutes each evening for a "talk time." That first evening, when the wife reminded her husband of their agreement, he looked up from his evening paper and said, "Fine, start talking." Obviously for communication to be effective, it must be mutual.

2. *Stay close to God and maintain an active religious faith*. The second most often mentioned key to marital success was the importance of retaining an active and vital religious faith. Such comments were quite prominent among traditionally evangelical Christians. Some spoke of the need to depend on God and turn to Him for direction, and others stressed that commitment to God and to His will fosters love and respect for one's spouse and a spirit of forgiveness so vital to a growing relationship.

3. *Build trust — act with honesty and integrity*. In commenting on the key to marital success, several Christiantowners mentioned honesty and trust. The two concepts are closely tied together and it is appropriate that they were often mentioned in the same phrase. People are inclined to be most honest with their mates when they have been faithful to their mate's trust. Conversely, it is hard for trust to develop when one mate knows that the other has been dishonest.

When a teenager complains about his parents' lack of trust, the parents are inclined to respond that the teenager must first demonstrate that he warrants their trust by acting honestly and responsibly. The same logic applies to the marriage relationship. But it is also possible for trust to foster honesty and integrity. When people know they have their spouses' trust, they tend to be less likely to violate it than when they believe they have no trust to lose.

4. *Exercise care and mutual concern*. One informant defined care as "commitment to the happiness of the other." Another defined it as a "willingness to give more than get." Both descriptions imply taking the other's welfare to heart. The caring relationship is such that when one partner aches, the other is very much aware of it and tries to ease the pain. Similarly, one partner's joy gives rise to mutual celebration.

5. *Strive to retain a sense of humor*. "Humor," noted one Christiantowner, "is the oil that lubricates the wheel; it helps prevent wear and tear." Another commented that when things look depressing and hopeless, humor helps put things into perspective. "Humor helps couples cope with the uncopeable."

Another study that sought to obtain marital advice from married couples was conducted by Sporakowski and Hughston (1978). In their inquiry they asked a sample of couples married fifty years or more to describe the ingredients for a happy marriage. We were intrigued to find that the first three themes which our couples mentioned also appeared in the first five responses given by the husbands and/or the wives in Sporakowski and Hughston's study. Thus the marriage insights that Christiantowners shared with us are not particularly unique to their community.

For the lessons derived from the experience of one generation to profit another, they must be communicated. Hopefully this chapter has facilitated such a transfer. Yet it is important that these lessons be applied in a way that fits the context of the times. In the next chapter we examine this context in terms of traditional and modern conceptions of marriage.

Chapter 11

Changing Sex Roles and Marriage Arrangements: Prospects for the Future

Maurine and Dennis Land have three children and are very much in love. Ben and Amy Carter also have three children and they, too, are in love, but at this point the similarity ends. The Lands and the Carters have chosen to organize their marriages in very different ways. Dennis Land has been intensively involved in the caring and nurturing of his children since Maurine returned from the hospital with their first child. In fact Dennis normally spent several hours a day feeding, changing, and playing with his young son and, more recently, with the couple's two young daughters. But Dennis' domestic involvement extends beyond child care. As Maurine explained, "During the week I watch the kids while Dennis does his plumbing work. When Dennis returns from work in the evening, he watches the kids while I work at the restaurant. On weekends we catch up on the housework. Dennis and I enjoy working around the house together. That's a special time for us."

Ben and Amy Carter have a more conventional arrangement. Ben believes that women are instinctively prepared to care for the kids and Amy readily agrees. Consequently Amy specializes in the domestic sphere, taking care of the home and the kids. She prides herself on being a good homemaker. For his part, Ben, who runs a farm equipment repair business, functions as income earner and money manager. As the husband, Ben is certain that his responsibilities and his competencies lie in these areas. In fact, Ben is convinced that the key to marital success lies in each pursuing his (or her) respective sphere of responsibility.

When asked, "What, if anything, do you wish you could share with your spouse?" Ben said that he wishes his wife could have a better understanding of the business world. He also wishes that she would enjoy activities like fishing and hunting. Amy echoed her husband's desire that they share more interests in common but wishes her husband would take her to plays and concerts, which Ben finds rather dull. Each claims to be in love with the other, but neither sees their marriage as a particularly happy one.

Maurine and Dennis Land have areas they would like to see changed as well. Early in their marriage the couple found themselves deep in debt. Their debt problems were aggravated by the early arrival of their first child and by some health problems that Maurine developed during her pregnancy. The Lands' financial woes had not attenuated much at the time of our interview, some nine years after the birth of their first child. Maurine, who manages the money and attends to the bills, told us, "I wish I could share some of these [financial] concerns with Dennis. But he gets so discouraged when I tell him about them." Dennis underscored the seriousness of their financial situation when he was asked what he thought would make life easier. "We've just begun to make some progress in paying our bills," he said. "Once we get our charge cards paid off, I'll rest a lot easier."

Because of their financial difficulties, the Lands have had to let their first car go back to the lender and nearly lost their house. Yet despite these adversities, both are quite pleased with their marriage and rate it as very happy. Both are convinced that much of their success lies in sharing so many of their interests and activities in common.

In recent years much debate has occurred over the merits of two divergent conceptions of how sex roles and marriage relationships should be patterned. One concept comes close to the way in which Ben and Amy Carter have structured their marriage. This traditionalist model of marriage has enjoyed popular support in past generations. Maurine and Dennis Land, on the other hand, reflect the modernist model of marriage, which challenges many of the assumptions implicit in the traditionalist model. In this chapter we will examine the extent to which Christiantowners conform to these contrasting models and the consequences these models have for the marriage relationship. First each model's assumptions and characteristics will be clarified.

THE TRADITIONALIST MODEL

Supporters of the traditionalist model maintain that several important and fundamental differences exist between the sexes. These differences are largely genetically determined and hence are not easily altered. Moreover, they are not merely physical but extend to reason and emotion as well. Men are believed, by nature, to be objective and rational in their approach to situations, and women are understood to be subjective and intuitive. Men are inclined to be aggressive, assertive, and competitive, and women are passive, submissive, and cooperative.

In past centuries the traits attributed to women have typically been viewed as far inferior to those attributed to men. This is nowhere more apparent than in Hebrew society during the period in which the books of the Bible were written. Sociologist and Bible scholar Donald Kraybill finds significance in the fact that the Hebrew adjectives for "pious," "just," and "holy" have no feminine form in the Old Testament. Kraybill goes on to observe that a negative view of women was also quite prevalent in New Testament society (Kraybill, 1980, pp. 403-405). Women were commonly considered to be liars, unreliable witnesses in court and unfit to receive religious instruction. During menstruation they were thought to be unclean and believed capable of polluting a holy place by their very presence.

This negative view of women extended into the early church. Church historian Pat Gundry cites passages typifying medieval thought concerning women:

> Thomas Aquinas, the father of medieval theology, said: As regards the individual nature, woman is defective and misbegotten, for the active force in the male seed tends to the production of a perfect likeness of the masculine sex; while the production of women comes from a defect in the active force or from some material indisposition, or even from some external influence, such as that of a south wind. . . .

Salimbene, a thirteenth-century Franciscan, said: "Woman was evil from the beginnings, a gate of death, a disciple of the servant, the devil's accomplice, a fount of deception, a dog-star to godly labours, rust corrupting the saints; whose perilous face hath overthrown such as had already become almost angels." (Gundry, 1980, p. 24)

Gundry maintains that much contemporary thinking about male and female differences is influenced by such medieval views. Perhaps the following statement by Ruth Graham, wife of evangelist Billy Graham, illustrates her point well. After listing a variety of areas in which she believes that men are superior to women, Mrs. Graham says, "You name it, men are superior in all but two areas: women make the best wives and women make the best mothers" (Graham, 1975).

To be fair, it should be pointed out that contemporary advocates of the traditionalist model are generally disinclined to regard women as negatively as in the past. Still, women are regarded by them as having traits and abilities which, while not to be regarded inferior, are nonetheless quite different and distinct from those possessed by men (Christenson, 1970, pp. 32-54).

In allocating marriage roles, traditionalists seek to honor the principle of complementarity. This principle asserts that marriage functions best when each sex, in the respective role of husband or wife, complements the talents and abilities of the other. A proper implementation of the functionality principle will result in happiness and harmony in the home and contribute to the well-being of society. Conversely, failure to respect the principle will lead to disharmony, disunity, and the breakdown of society (Elliot, 1989).

In keeping with this principle, the traditionalist model calls for a clear, sex-based division of labor. Normally the model assumes that the husband will shoulder the responsibility of the provider role. As the husband, he is the one best qualified to perform heavy work, attend to technical tasks, and represent his family in external affairs. Because of his capacity for reason and objectivity, he is the appropriate one to assume authority for making major decisions, financial and otherwise. And because he is instinctively sexually aggressive, it is assumed that he will take the initiative in this area as well.

The wife's role must complement her husband's by centering around the domestic sphere. The wife is the appropriate one to look after the house, care for the children, do the shopping, prepare the meals, and remember Aunt Martha's birthday.

Support for the Traditionalist Approach

The traditional model of marriage has long been the object of some folk wisdom, but the approach has found additional support in the social sciences and in theology as well. A good example of support from the social science community is evident in the writing of Parsons and Bales (1955). In their study of small groups, these investigators discerned two types of leadership. One type, which Parsons and Bales call the "instrumental leader," helps to clarify group goals while directing the group toward accomplishing its objectives. A second type, the "socio-emotional leader," functions to hold the group together by seeing that immediate needs are taken care of and that the group functions as a cohesive social unit. Both kinds of leadership, Parsons and Bales maintain, are of vital importance to a group. Yet rarely is one person able to perform both leadership roles.

In marriage, a special kind of group, the instrumental leader's role has traditionally been assumed by the husband and the socio-emotional role has been assumed by the wife (Pleck, 1979). This arrangement, so the logic goes, serves in the interest of marital (group) harmony, stability, and efficiency.

Arguments in support of the traditional model of marriage have come from theologians operating in the tradition of Thomas Aquinas and Martin Luther (Jewett, 1975, pp. 61-86). Just as God equipped woman to bear and to nurse children, they argue, so He equipped man with the strength and ability to provide for his wife and children (Jewett, 1975, p. 61-86).

In matters of authority, these theologians support a hierarchical order of creation which sets God above man and man over woman (LaHaye & LaHaye, 1976; Christenson, 1970). In marriage, so their analogy goes, the husband is to derive his strength and direction from God while the wife is to derive her value and direction from her husband.

THE MODERNIST MODEL

A second view of the sexes stresses the underlying similarity of men and women. According to this approach, most observed differences are not so much the result of some genetic coding as the product of social conditioning. In actuality the needs, potentials, and proclivities of the sexes are understood to approximate each other rather than simply to complement one another. This approach to sex roles and the marriage arrangement derived from it is the modernist approach.[1]

When it comes to marriage, modernists stress two principles: (a) role flexibility and (b) role sharing. In accordance with the first principle, interest and ability should take precedence over gender in determining appropriate role assignment. Couples function best when they avoid getting locked into fixed gender-specific roles. Dissatisfaction and role-estrangement occur, they warn, when individuals are coerced into assuming a role just because of their gender. In marriage, couples must strive to tailor their roles to their unique needs and abilities, irrespective of how unconventional or countertraditional the emerging arrangement may be.

The second principle, role sharing, emphasizes the value to be derived from sharing roles in common. Role sharing, modernists allege, facilitates mutual appreciation of, empathy for, and companionship with one's mate. Role segregation, on the other hand, frustrates the development of true companionship. The husband who helps his wife with the shopping, the housework, and the baby's two o'clock feeding comes to a better understanding and appreciation of his wife by sharing these roles with her. Similarly, the wife who joins her husband in the labor force expands her capacity to understand and appreciate her husband. Crossing traditional sex-role boundaries has the added advantage of facilitating the experience of a range of emotions and the recognition of capacities which would otherwise remain unappreciated and dormant.

Like the traditionalists, the modernists have found support for their position in both the social sciences and theology. Social scientists DeJong and Wilson (1979) understand the traditional approach to sex roles and marriage organization as previously a matter of practical necessity. It emerged, they suggest, at a time when death rates were high and the need for manual labor was great. Under these conditions, bearing and rearing children were considered of utmost importance. Consequently the role of the woman as wife became synonymous with motherhood while the protector/provider role necessarily fell to the husband. In time, stereotypes concerning the nature of men and women emerged to legitimize the arrangement and insure that the sexes would be channeled into the roles considered most functional for family, tribal and clan welfare.

DeJong and Wilson point out that the momentum of support for traditional sex stereotypes persists to the present time, but today's circumstances are radically different from what they were in the past. Consequently, DeJong and Wilson call for a fresh approach to gender and marriage roles in keeping with the structure of today's society.

A second social science approach understands sex roles and sex-role stereotypes as having originated as a means for coping with value inconsistencies in society. A proponent of this approach, Randi Gunther (1976), observes that Western culture stresses the value of competition, but also the virtue of cooperation. People learn that it is important to stand up for their rights but also to show respect for authority. They are urged to be winners but to feel sorry for the losers. They are encouraged to be aggressive leaders but also to be dutiful followers.

According to Gunther, the solution that Western culture has developed to resolve these conflicts is to attribute one set of value characteristics to men and another set of conflicting value characteristics to women. Thus traits such as competition and aggression are stressed in males while cooperation and passivity are stressed in females. Parents, and others who mold children into culturally appropriate adults, have so internalized these gender-appropriate values that they take great pains to reproduce them in each new generation. As young boys act out aggression, they are praised for being "all boy." Girls, on the other hand, are praised for being neat and quiet "little ladies."

To avoid social disapproval, boys learn that they must be strong and suppress, even repress from consciousness, certain "feminine" inclinations such as tears. Girls, on the other hand, learn that they must repress masculine inclinations, such as being too pushy. Here is where a major problem emerges, says Gunther. In repressing the socially unacceptable masculine or feminine parts of their natures, men and women fail to become whole and complete human beings. And, as psychoanalysts are prone to point out, such repression leads to self-estrangement, impulse denial, and projecting unacceptable tendencies in oneself onto the opposite sex. (This latter inclination at times leads to criticizing members of the opposite sex for manifesting these characteristics.) Traditional sex and marriage roles perpetuate the problem and thereby insure a measure of alienation between the sexes. The principles of role flexibility and role sharing are put forward as two solutions to this problem. Both serve to facilitate self-acceptance in the individual and companionship in marriage.

Christian theologians who support the modernist model of marriage point out that scripture makes little reference to masculine and feminine characteristics. When Jesus spoke of spiritual maturity (e.g., Matthew 5-7), and when Paul spoke of the fruits of the spirit (Galatians 5:22,23), neither made any mention of a feminine or masculine application. This is also true in the Pauline passage from Galatians 3:28: "There is neither . . . male nor female; for you are all one in Christ Jesus." The Biblical characters Deborah or Phoebe violated the sex-role stereotypes of the day, and Priscilla and Aquila, a Greek couple referred to in Scripture (Acts 18) shared their work role together (Scanzoni, 1979).

WHICH MODEL OF MARRIAGE
DO CHRISTIANTOWNERS FOLLOW?

Virtually all of the husbands we interviewed were working and most functioned as the primary income provider in the marriage. Most husbands had considerably more formal education than their wives; roughly equivalent numbers of husbands and wives had some college education but when it came to holding graduate degrees, husbands outnumbered wives three to one. Christiantown men also tended to marry women somewhat younger than themselves. The average age at marriage for men and for women was 24.8 and 23.6 years, respectively. While this may reflect the additional time that men feel they must take before marriage in order to become adequate providers, a husband's older age is nonetheless consistent with male dominance and, in this sense, with the traditional model of marriage (Weeks, 1989, p. 289).

In contrast to their husbands, only half of the Christiantown wives we interviewed were employed, and only a little over one-third of these (36%) were employed full-time. The majority of the women focused most of their attention on the domestic role. Although husbands of working wives tend to render greater assistance in child care than husbands whose wives were unemployed, women still spend the greater amount of time caring for the children (cf. Krausz, 1986).

Despite their traditional work roles, Christiantowners most conform to the modernist model of marriage. In fact, there is considerable evidence of role flexibility and role sharing. Wives are the primary money managers about as often as the husbands. And, as we have observed, when women do work, their husbands are inclined to share in the child care.

There is evidence of other shared activity as well. Husbands and wives both report discussing major financial expenditures together and, when either spouse receives extra income, regarding this income as the property of both. In the case of sex, we have noted that while the husband assumes a more aggressive role in some marriages, in a number of other marriages the husband and wife share this role equally. In light of such variation, to classify all Christiantown couples as operating in the traditional mode would be misleading.

Education and Wives

The results of numerous studies attest to the positive impact of education on the marriage relationship (Burr, 1976, pp. 239-240). The logical explanation appears to be that better educated spouses are more capable of articulating their feelings and understanding the other sex.[2]

Our evidence suggests that the beneficial effects of education on the marriage relationship derive more from the husband's education than from the wife's. When we examined the correspondence between husband's education and wife's marital adjustment we found that the two were positively related — as a husband's education increased so did his wife's marital adjustment (Figure 11.1). But when we checked to see whether husband's marital adjustment was similarly related to the level of his wife's education, we failed to find any discernible relationship. Another interesting pattern which we observed is that the marital happiness and satisfaction of wives is more affected by their husbands' education than by their own.

Why should a husband's education be so closely related to his wife's marital adjustment, but not the other way around? One possible explanation is that education bolsters the authority of the husband and thus further legitimates, in the mind of his wife, his traditional role as head of the house. This logic may explain why the relationship is so one-sided. But if it holds true, then we would expect that a wife's marital adjustment will improve as her husband's education increases relative to her own. Yet we found no evidence of such improvement.

Perhaps the real reason for the difference has less to do with the way wives respond to educated husbands than to the fact that education, for the man, closely corresponds to both his occupational sta-

FIGURE 11.1 Wife's Marital Adjustment by Husband's Education Level

```
======================================================================

Husband's Education                 Percent with Above Average
   (number)                              Marital Adjustment
----------------------------------------------------------------------


High School          ******************* 40%
   (n=10)

College              ******************************. 63%
   (n=11)

Graduate School      *******************************************. 83%
   (n=29)
----------------------------------------------------------------------
```

Kruskal-Wallis H = 6.61; p = ≤ .04

tus and to the size of his income. And, as we have previously noted, both of these are related to a wife's marital adjustment.

WHICH MARRIAGE MODEL WORKS BEST?

One of the earliest and most cited studies of marriage organization and marital satisfaction was conducted by the Lynds in 1924 and 1925, and again in 1935. In their Muncie, Indiana study, the Lynds found strong evidence of what we have termed the traditional approach to marriage. They also found that couples who conformed most closely to the traditional sex and marriage role pattern also experienced a low level of marital companionship. Communication was poor and social interaction, particularly outside the home, was infrequent. Couples tended to have few friends in common and, except for some bridge parties and church gatherings, did few things together. Among couples in this situation, the Lynds found few happy marriages (Lynd & Lynd, 1939).

What about Christiantown couples? Does the traditional marriage pattern impede companionship for them today as it apparently did for the Lynds' couples over a half century ago? And does the modernist model of marriage do a better job of cultivating marital adjustment?

To answer this question we must single out some criterion by which to distinguish between couples who conform to the traditionalist model of marriage and those who conform to the modernist model, and then compare the respective marriages. Perhaps the single best criterion for distinguishing between the two types is the way in which couples make decisions. To help assess how Christiantowners make decisions, we asked our respondents to think of a subject over which they most often disagree with their mate. The majority said "money" or "finances." We then asked them to indicate whether they typically resolve the issue through mutual agreement or by one or the other partner's giving in. Those couples who typically resolve the issue by mutual agreement would, in sharing the decision-making role, be manifesting a modernist marriage pattern. Those in which the wife typically gives in would be conforming more closely to the traditional pattern. (Those in which the husband gives in would technically conform to neither pattern.)

To assess the consequences of these patterns for marital well-being, we computed the percentage of respondents conforming to each mode of decision-making who (a) scored above average on our communication/companionship index (Figure 3.1) and (b) scored above average on our marital adjustment index (Appendix A, Table A.7). As is apparent from Figure 11.2, spouses who resolve marital conflict by mutual give-and-take (the modernist pattern) are significantly more likely to enjoy above-average communication and companionship than are spouses who cope with conflict by the wife's giving in (the traditional pattern) or by the husband's giving in. This finding may not be too surprising since the mutual give-and-take pattern would seem to require a good amount of communication and this in turn might logically result in a fair degree of companionship.

When it comes to marital adjustment, some interesting contrasts appear. For one thing, the number of spouses conforming to the "husband gives in" or to the "wife gives in" pattern is the same, but the incidence of above-average adjustment is by far the lowest for the former group. This pattern, as we have noted, conforms to neither the traditionalist nor the modernist models of marriage. In fact it probably brings to mind stereotypical images of the henpecked husband. Perhaps the reason why this decision-making pat-

FIGURE 11.2. Level of Companionship According to pattern employed in resolving greatest disagreement

Mode of Conflict Resolution (number)	Percentage with Above Average Communication/Companionship
Husband Giving In (N=14)	********************. 43%
Wife Giving In (N=14)	***************** 36%
Mutual Agreement (N=64)	*********************************. 69%

Chi square (2df.) = 7.18; p = ≤ .05

tern is so poorly associated with good (above average) adjustment is due to the strong social sentiment against it.

A comparison of Figures 11.2 and 11.3 reveals a second difference. Whereas spouses who typically resolve conflict by mutual agreement are more inclined to have above-average communication and companionship scores, those following the traditional pattern (wife gives in) are somewhat more likely to enjoy above-average marital adjustment. Why this difference? Why might those who opt for a modernist approach find it more difficult to achieve a high degree of marital adjustment? Perhaps the reason has to do with the difficulty of coming to grips with change (Szinovacs, 1984).

MEETING CHANGE

A number of social forces are coalescing to move couples further away from the traditionalist model of marriage and closer to the modernist model. The growing momentum of the women's movement has encouraged women, and some men, to explore new roles, both within marriage and without. Sexual interest and aggression on the part of women are becoming more legitimate. Each decade sees progressively higher percentages of wives and mothers joining their

FIGURE 11.3. Level of Marital Adjustment according to pattern employed for resolving greatest disagreement

```
================================================================
Mode of Conflict Resolution      Percentage with Above Average
    (number)                           Marital Adjustment
----------------------------------------------------------------

Husband Giving In
    (n=14)            **********. 21%

Wife Giving In
    (n=14)            ******************************** 64%

Mutual Agreement
    (n=64)            ************************* . 53%

----------------------------------------------------------------
```

Kruskal-Wallis H = 6.61; p = ≤ .04

husbands in the work force, and today's college women are increasingly committed to pursuing high status professional careers while seeking satisfaction from leadership, prestige, and esteem (Regan & Roland, 1985).

Partially as a consequence of these changes, today's Christiantown couples are opting to share more roles and to join in the decision-making process. This poses quite a contrast from the situation which existed just a generation ago. For example, 65% of Christiantown couples report that when it comes to the issue over which they disagree most often, they resolve the issue by mutual give-and-take, i.e., the modernist pattern. (Eighty-five percent said they typically resolve all disagreements in this way.) In contrast, less than one-third (31%) of their parents resolved disagreements in this way, from reports by Christiantowners of their parents' behavior.

The rapidity of this change has confronted the current generation of couples wishing to incorporate a modernist model of marriage with certain problems. In many, if not most, cases, such couples were raised in families that conformed to the traditional pattern. As a consequence they are now faced with having to incorporate an emerging ideal in the absence of parental role models to demonstrate precisely how to share in the decision-making process and household chores, and to attend to a myriad of other details that must be worked out (Hiller & Philliber, 1986).

Another problem arises from the emphasis the modernist model places on the principle of role flexibility in which role responsibilities in marriage are assumed on the basis of interest and ability independent of one's gender. No longer can a couple simply assume that the husband will work outside the home while the wife takes care of the house, does the laundry, and functions as babysitter and nurse maid. No longer can either spouse assume that the wife will gladly prepare dinner or wash the dishes while the husband relaxes in his easy chair reading the evening paper. Rather, the modernist model requires that couples somehow assess each other's strengths and weaknesses, interests and idiosyncrasies, and channel these into a workable and mutually satisfying arrangement. Moreover they must often do this without guidelines to assist them in the process.

The difficulty of this undertaking is underscored by Maximiliane

Szinovacs (1984). In her research review, she found that although many couples' attitudes toward role flexibility and role sharing had shifted toward what we have termed the modernist model, the actual implementation of these attitudes in day-to-day life has met with marginal success. Thus while many husbands espouse the idea of sharing "female" tasks in the household (cleaning, cooking, and child care), their actual participation in these areas is still considered optional. The responsibility for performing such tasks still rests primarily on wives. This discrepancy between professed attitudes and actual behavior may account for many of the difficulties encountered by Christiantown couples attempting to implement modernist ideals. In light of these difficulties, we might well understand why Christiantown couples who conform to the modernist mode are experiencing somewhat lower levels of marital adjustment.

NOTES

1. The "modernist" approach has much in common with the feminist perspective but because of mixed messages conveyed by the term "feminist," we have opted for the present term. Many of my students have, upon commenting in class, prefaced their remarks by the statement, "I'm not a feminist, but . . ." and then proceeded to endorse a basically feminist position.

2. An exception to Burr's principle is noted by Levande, Koch, & Koch (1983, pp. 468-9) who report that the higher the education attained by the spouses, the lower their satisfaction with marriage. They suggest that the higher educated people are inclined to be more critical of their performance as husbands and wives.

3. Szinovacz (1984) also reminds us that while employment for wives and mothers is generally accepted, women are rarely fully responsible for the economic support of the household. The economic support of the family is still regarded by most people as appropriately the husband's primary responsibility.

Chapter 12

Assessment and Application:
Toward a Constructive Response

Throughout this book we have been focusing on the many factors that influence the marriage relationship in Christiantown. Despite what critics may say, Christiantowners, on the whole, experience above-average levels of marital happiness and adjustment.[1] It is possible that this reflects in part their success in other areas. As we have noted, Christiantowners enjoy above-average levels of income, education, occupational status, and home ownership—the kinds of advantages which many assume make up "the good life."[2] However impressive these overall averages appear, it is important to keep in mind that our Christiantown respondents manifest a fair amount of diversity, not only in education, income, and occupational status, but also in religiosity and quality of their marriage. This diversity has permitted us to investigate how variations in one area, e.g., occupational status, correspond to variations in other areas, e.g., marital happiness and marital adjustment.

When Christiantowners comment on what they find to be the most satisfactory aspects of their marriages, companionship or some variant thereof is mentioned more often than any other aspect. Some sociologists have suggested that companionship in marriage has special significance in the context of modern society (Burgess, Locke, & Thomas, 1971) But irrespective of the extent to which this has replaced other values, one thing seems clear: insofar as Christiantowners experience companionship in their marriages, they are likely to find them satisfying. Consequently those concerned with promoting marital well-being, be it in their own relationship or in others, will want to encourage those factors which contribute to marital companionship.

In Chapter 5 we noted a close association between companionship and sexual satisfaction. The simple act of doing things together, like playing a game, taking a walk, or working on a joint project, may significantly improve companionship and, in so doing, improve the sexual relationship. In some respects, this is one of the easier remedies to follow.

As we have seen in Chapter 5, sexual satisfaction also improves as sex becomes a mutually shared activity. Obviously there are times when either partner will be more sexually receptive than the other, but sexual satisfaction tends to be greatest when couples obtain a balance in their expression of sexual passion. A variety of beliefs (e.g., that sex has little to do with love) and behaviors (e.g., seeking sexual gratification without considering the needs or wishes of one's spouse) can prevent sex from becoming a mutually shared and mutually gratifying activity. By removing these barriers, couples can experience a significant improvement in their sexual relationship.

In the latter part of our chapter on marital sex we noted the positive correspondence between husbands' occupational status and their sexual satisfaction. This association might imply that raising a husband's occupational status is a good way to improve the sexual relationship. But occupational status reflects the conditions of his employment and the people with whom he associates. It is toward these areas, and the attitudes which emerge from them, that attention needs to be directed. Couples and counselors may have to take a close look at these circumstances and, when necessary, work on appropriate changes.

Given the stress which Christiantown couples place on companionship, we were curious to note what they would most like to see changed in their marriage. Many mentioned a desire for more time together, more money, or both. Time and money are closely connected and inversely related commodities. For most people, the situation is such that money must first be earned for one to afford time off. Yet the more time one spends at leisure, the more one's financial survival is jeopardized. In the next few paragraphs we will consider some of the implications of our findings with regard to money and how it is earned.

In some respects, Christiantowners appear to enjoy considerable financial companionship. The majority report that they discuss major family expenditures and most indicate that they share their respective incomes in common. Yet from what Christiantowners told us, money is by far their most frequent source of disagreement. What makes conflicts over money particularly difficult to resolve are the subjective feelings and symbolic meanings people attach to it.

As couples seek to resolve their disagreements over money and its use, they need to be aware of the subjective significance the issue carries in the mind of each partner. At this point counselors and others desiring to facilitate marital well-being can provide valuable assistance by enabling spouses to become more aware of their personal thoughts and feelings about money as well as their origin and intensity. Having done this, couples may also need assistance in communicating these to one another, which may be quite difficult until such attitudes become acceptable both to oneself and to one's spouse.

Counselors also need to keep in mind the potential impact that income has on a wife's marital adjustment and satisfaction. Although she may not be completely aware of it, dissatisfaction with income and the lifestyle it dictates may adversely affect the wife's contentment with both her marriage and her spouse. Consequently it may be especially important for wives to clarify their feelings about income and process these feelings appropriately.

When considering the means by which husbands endeavor to earn money, we noted that Christiantown husbands have experienced a significant increase in occupational status compared to their fathers. While this has come at the expense of hard work for some, career mobility does not appear to have seriously jeopardized the well-being of the marriage relationship. On the contrary, our indicators of marital well-being reveal that the wives of high-status husbands are better off than their lower-status counterparts.

A husband's work satisfaction also appears to affect the marriage relationship, though in a somewhat inconsistent way. Whereas husbands who are dissatisfied with their work appear to turn to their wives sexually, possibly as a means of compensating for their feelings of dissatisfaction, they are somewhat less inclined to engage their wives in meaningful discussions or to spend time with them in other ways. Our data suggest that the reason may relate to the lack of gratification they experience when attempting to do so.

Counselors and other family life facilitators need to be sensitive to this issue. Husbands may need to examine how their work attitudes impact their marriage. In some instances, they may need counseling in how to share their work-related feelings with their wives. Conversely, wives may need guidance in how to anticipate their husbands' feelings and how to handle these as they are shared. Wives who are particularly dependent on their husbands for their own sense of well-being may need special assistance in handling any self-blame they may experience over their husbands' frustrations or feelings of failure.

The increase in the number and proportion of wives and mothers in the labor force was noted in Chapter 8. This represents one of the most revolutionary changes to impact the family in the latter half of this century. Because of the rapidity of the change and the lack of clear guidelines to cope with it, dual-earner couples may experience some strain in their marriage relationship. Those who work with married couples and their families need to be alert to the unique kinds of problems likely to confront them. They also must be prepared to offer assistance in devising suitable coping strategies. For example, couples may need special guidance in allocating domestic responsibilities in a timely and mutually satisfying manner. And, lest employed wives be put in a no-win situation, it is important that husbands develop a capacity to recognize the contribution their wives are making, even when the latter's absence from the home requires extra work for the husbands.

How religion affects the marriage relationship is a question that has spawned considerable debate. Some critics have warned that religion can have harmful effects. Much of their concern revolves around the conviction that conservative Christian beliefs foster an exploitative pattern of husband-dominance and wife-submission (McNamara, 1984). As we noted in Chapter 4, the vast majority of Christians who hold to a conservative set of religious beliefs are convinced that the Bible indeed teaches that a wife should submit to her husband's authority. But we found virtually no evidence that this conviction is actually linked to a pattern of husband-dominance and wife-submission. The case of Mat and Emily Bradley, referred to at the outset of Chapter 4, may conform to the husband-dominant stereotype, but their situation does not conform to the rule, at least among Christiantowners.

For those who would tout the beneficial effects of religion on the marriage relationship, a word of caution may be in order. We failed to find a correspondence between our measures of marital well-being (marital happiness, adjustment, and companionship) and the traditional manifestations of religiosity (the experience of spiritual salvation, commitment to God, prayer, church attendance, and the upholding of conservative beliefs). We did find, though, that the more conservative people's religious beliefs and the more frequent their church attendance, the less inclined they are to consider divorce as an option. A commitment to marital stability, of itself, does not insure a good marriage.

There are two areas in which religion proved to be significantly related to marriage. One is in the area of tithing. The more regularly people report giving a percentage of their income to a church or to other religious causes, the greater their marital happiness and the higher their marital adjustment. Yet this relationship must be interpreted carefully. It seems questionable that by regularly giving money to religious causes, a couple whose marriage is in trouble will suddenly experience an improvement in their relationship. Such couples might be better advised to consider marital counseling, perhaps by utilizing a church-subsidized service while donating the subsidy to a religious cause.

Fertility is a second area where religion seems to have an impact. Interestingly, the more conservative one's religious beliefs, the more children one is likely to have. Some have suggested that this "fertility factor" helps to explain much of the numerical growth of doctrinally conservative churches (Bibby & Brinkerhoff, 1973). When paired with the growing number of employed mothers, this fertility may also help explain the popularity of church-sponsored day-care centers (Crow, 1986).

Conservative believers are not only inclined to have larger numbers of children, but as parents they are very concerned that their children develop a personal and right relationship with God. The sustained popularity of Christian schools is one manifestation of this concern. Indeed, any program or activity which purports to further this objective will likely meet with a warm reception.

The level of life satisfaction is inclined to reach a low ebb during the years when preschool children are present. Counselors and family service providers need to be alert to signs of parental stress and depression during this time. Couples with several (three or more) children may need special assistance in managing their time and their responsibilities.

During these formative years, parents would do well to assess their child-rearing motives and the impact these motives are having on both them and their children. Self-oriented parents, whose ego needs require that their children measure up to their parents' expectations and satisfy their needs, may need to become more child-centered. Conversely, child-centered parents may need help in recognizing the legitimacy of meeting their own needs and not just those of their children.

Finally, all parents may benefit from assistance in clarifying their ultimate child-rearing goals and the means for obtaining them, particularly in terms of achieving a proper balance between developing in their children a healthy self-regard and a responsible concern for the welfare of others.

Insofar as it is possible to profit from the experience of others, the lessons learned by Christiantowners may prove helpful. The experience of Christiantowners suggests that couples often fail to get to know one another's faults and weak points before they marry. It also indicates that couples frequently tend to over-romanticize marriage. A number of our Christiantowners learned the hard way that marriage, to be successful, requires a realignment of priorities. The extent to which this may be necessary and the way in which required realignment is to be accomplished needs to be the subject of premarital counseling. Christiantowners also point out that communication is vital to the maintenance of a healthy marriage. Any obstacles to self-disclosure need to be overcome. Couples also must learn to recognize the early warning signals of impending conflict and know how to take appropriate action to correct the situation. Finally, if couples can recognize that problems occur even in the best of marriages, and among the best of people, they may stand a better chance of overcoming pride and obtaining necessary outside assistance.

Outside assistance occasionally comes from other parenting couples. In an effort to find ways to cope with the responsibilities of housework and child care, some Christiantown women banned together to form an informal neighborhood network. These women take turns watching each others' kids, carpooling, exchanging trips to the grocery store, and providing general assistance with a host of other activities.

In some instances these networks have been formalized into shopping cooperatives, tool and machine exchanges, and nursery school services. Such formalization has the advantage of increasing the dependability and longevity of vital services which make shouldering family responsibilities more manageable. Since today's couples are often isolated from family and kin, such networks provide a ready resource to call on when emergencies arise.

All self-help and professional assistance efforts must be done in the context of changing sex roles and marriage models. As we saw in the last chapter, a modern model of marriage is replacing the more traditional model. This change poses new problems and challenges. Christiantown couples who have attempted to appropriate the new model experience below-average marital adjustment and marital happiness scores. These barometers of marital well-being indicate that these couples are having some difficulty making the transition. Yet to the extent that the modernist model is becoming the popularly accepted ideal, there is room for optimism. As the current generation of children moves into marriage, many of them will have grown up with fathers and mothers who make joint decisions, share household and child-rearing tasks, and so on. In short, they will have had parental role models to instruct them in how to negotiate and construct a modern marriage.

In the meantime, marriage counselors and other family life facilitators can play a critical role in helping couples clarify their own model of marriage, examining the model's implications, and implementing it to the satisfaction of those concerned. Insofar as these resource persons and couples themselves correctly anticipate and productively respond to the demands confronting them in the context of contemporary society, they can be said to possess the keys to successful marriage.

NOTES

1. It is also possible that the appearance of overall marital well-being is favorably affected by our sampling procedure. Only people in intact marriages and those in marriages which survived long enough to see at least one child in grade school were selected for inclusion in our sample. And there were some couples who were selected for inclusion in our sample that chose not to cooperate. These possibilities should be considered when attempting to generalize our findings beyond Christiantown.

2. In these respects, Christiantown stands apart from the Lynds' "Middletown," Kamarovsky's "Glenton," and Blood and Wolfe's study of the Detroit area.

References

CHAPTER 1

Blood, R. O., & Wolfe, D. M. (1960). *Husbands & Wives: The Dynamics of Married Living*. New York: Free Press.

Church proposes a divorce vow. (1976, November 9). *Chicago Tribune*, p. 9.

Gans, H. (1962). *The Urban Villagers*. New York: Free Press.

Gans, H. J. (1967). *The Levittowners: Ways of Life and Politics in a New Suburban Community*. New York: Pantheon.

Gruner, L. (1985). The correlation of private, religious devotional practices and marital adjustment. *Journal of Comparative Family Studies 16* (1), 47-59.

Hadden, J. K. (1983). Televangelism and the mobilization of a new Christian right family policy. In W. D. D'Antoni, W.D., & J. Aldous (Eds.). *Families and Religions* (pp. 247-266). Beverly Hills: Sage.

Hollingshead, A. B. (1949). *Elmtown's Youth: The Impact of Social Class on Adolescents*. New York: John Wiley.

Komarovsky, M. (1962). *Blue-collar Marrige*. New York: Random House.

Larsen, J. A. (1978). Dysfunction in the evangelical family: Treatment considerations. *The Family Coordinator 27* (3), 261-265.

Lynd, R. S., & Lynd, H. M. (1929). *Middletown: A Study in Contemporary Culture*. New York: Harcourt, Brace.

Lynd, R. S., & Lynd, H. M. (1937). *Middletown in Transition: A Study in Cultural Conflicts*. New York: Harcourt, Brace & World.

McNamara, P.H. (1985a). The new Christian right's view of the family and its social science critics: A study in differing presuppositions. *Journal of Marriage and the Family 47* (2), 449-458.

McNamara, P.H. (1985b). Conservative Christian families and their moral world: Some reflections for sociologists. *Sociological Analysis 46* (2), 93-99.

Mace, D. & Mace, V. (1974). *We Can Have Better Marriages – If We Really Want Them*. Nashville: Abingdon

Peters, G. L. & Larkin, R. P. (1983) *Population geography: Problems, concepts, and prospects* (2nd ed.). Dubuque, Iowa: Kendal/Hunt (pp. 248, 250).

Scanzoni, J. (1983). *Shaping Tomorrow's Family: Theory and Policy for the 21st Century*. Beverly Hills: Sage.

U.S. Bureau of the Census. (1988) *County and City Data Book, 1988*. Washington, D.C.: U.S. Government Printing Office.

Warner, W. L. (1963). *Yankee City*. New Haven, Conn.: Yale University Press.

CHAPTER 2

Greater Wheaton Chamber of Commerce (1985). *Wheaton, Illinois* Unpublished document.

U.S. Bureau of the Census (1988). *County and City Data Book, 1988.* Washington, D.C.: U.S. Government Printing Office.

CHAPTER 3

Bernard, J. (1972). *The Future of Marriage.* New York: World Press.

Burgess, E. W., Locke, H. J., & Thomas, M. M. (1971) *The Family: From Tradition to Companionship* (4th ed.). New York: Van Nostrand Reinhold.

Barling, J. (1984). Effects of husbands' work experiences on wives' marital satisfaction. *The Journal of Social Psychology 124*, 219-225.

Caplow, T., Bahr, H. M., Chadwick, B. A., Hill, R., & Williamson, M. H. (1982). *Middletown Families: Fifty Years of Continuity and Change.* St. Paul, MN: University of Minnesota Press (p. 368).

Dolmatch, T. B. (Ed.). (1980) *Information Please Almanac.* (p. 803). New York: Simon and Schuster.

Fowers, B. J. & Olson, D. H. (1968). Predicting marital success with PREPARE: A predictive validity study. *Journal of Marital and Family Therapy, 12*, 403-413.

Goode, W. (1970) *World Revolution and Family Patterns.* New York: The Free Press (pp. 27-86).

Gove, W. R. (1972). The relationship between sex roles, marital status, and mental illness. *Social Forces 51*, 34-44.

Holloway, D. (1987) *Living and working together: The reality of two-generation farm families.* Unpublished master's thesis, Montana State University, Bozeman, MT.

Leslie, G. (1982). *The Family in Social Context* (5th ed.). New York: Oxford. (p. 449).

Locke, H. J., & Wallace, K. M. (1959). Short marital adjustment and prediction tests: Their reliability and validity. *Marriage and Family Living*, 21, 251-255.

Miller, B. C. (1976). A multivariate developmental model of marital satisfaction. *Journal of Marriage and the Family* 38, 643-657.

O'Leary, K. D., & Turkewitz, H. (1978). Methodological errors in marital and child treatment research. *Journal of Consulting Clinical Psychology 46*, 747-758.

Orthner, D. K. (1975) Leisure activity patterns and marital satisfaction over the marital career. *Journal of Marriage and the Family 37*, 91-101.

Spanier, G. (1976). Measuring dyadic adjustment: New scales for assessing the quality of marriage and similar dyads. *Journal of Marriage and the Family 36*, 15-28.

Sporakowski, M. J. & Hughston, G. A. (1978). Perceptions for happy marriage:

Adjustments and satisfactions of couples married for fifty or more years. *The Family Coordinator 27*, 321-327.

Wexler, B. (1980, May 23). Village of the saved *Reader: Chicago's Free Weekly*, pp. 39-40.

CHAPTER 4

Blumstein, P. & Schwartz, P. (1983). *American Couples: Money, Work, Sex*. New York: William Morrow.

Caplow, T., Bahr, H. M., Chadwick, B. A., Hill, R., & Williamson, M. H. (1982). Middletown Families: Fifty Years of Continuity and Change. St. Paul, MN: University of Minnesota Press (p. 368).

Christenson, L. (1970). *The Christian Family*. Minneapolis, MN: Bethany Fellowship.

Gallup Organization, The (1984). *Religion in America: The Gallup Report*. Princeton, N. J.: Princeton Religious Research Center (p. 58.).

Gruner, L. (1985). The correlation of private religious devotional practices and marital adjustment. *Journal of Comparative Family Studies 16* (1), 47-59.

Hadden, J. K. (1983). Televangelism and the mobilization of a new Christian right family policy, pp. 247-266 in D'Antonio, W.D., & Aldous, J. (eds.). *Families and Religion*. Beverly Hills: Sage.

Hunt, R. A., & King, M. B. (1978). Religiosity and marriage. *Journal for the Scientific Study of Religion 17* (4), 399-406.

Hunter, J. D. (1983). *American Evangelicalism: Conservative Religion and the Quandry of Modernity*. New Brunswick: Rutgers University Press.

LaHaye, T. & LaHaye, B. (1976). *The Act of Marriage*. Grand Rapids, MI: Zondervan.

McNamara, P. A. (1985b). Conservative Christian families and their moral world: Some reflections for sociologists. *Sociological Analysis 46* (2), 93-99.

Scanzoni, J. (1983). *Shaping Tomorrow's Family: Theory and Policy for the 21st Century*. Beverly Hills: Sage.

Stark, R. & Glock C. Y. (1970). *American Piety: The Nature of Religious Commitment*. Berkeley: University of California Press (pp. 57-80).

Stellway, R. J. (1973). The correspondence between religious orientation and socio-political liberalism and conservatism. *Sociological Quarterly 14*, 530-539.

Stellway, R. J. (1976). Social support and the socio-political consequences of two religious belief orientations. *Indian Journal of Comparative Sociology 2*, 32-40.

Tomasson, R. F. (1970). *Sweden: Prototype of Modern Society*. New York: Random House (p. 61).

CHAPTER 5

Bahr, S. J. (1989). *Family Interaction*. New York: MacMillan.

Banmen, J., & Vogel, N. A. (1985). The relationship between marital quality and interpersonal sexual communication. *Family Therapy 12* (1), 45-58.

Bellah, R., Madsen, R., Sullivan, W. M., Swindler, A., & Topton, S. M. (1985). *Habits of the Heart: Individualism and Commitment in American Life*. Berkeley, CA: University of California Press (p. 87).

Blumstein, P., & Schwartz, P. (1983). *American Couples*. New York: William Morrow.

Burns, A. (1984). Perceived cause of marriage breakdown and conditions of life. *Journal of Marriage and the Family 46* (August), 551-562.

Ehrmann, W. W. (1959). *Premarital Dating Behavior*. New York: Holt, Rinehart, and Winston (pp. 144-145).

Gaesser, D. L., & Whitbourne, S. K. (1985). Work identity and marital adjustment in blue-collar men. *Journal of Marriage and the Family 47* (3), 747-751.

General Social Survey (1987). Raw data supplied by NORC, a Social Science Research Center, Chicago, IL.

Grauerholz, E., & Serpe, R. T. (1985). Initiation and response: The dynamics of sexual interaction. *Sex Roles 12*:1041-1059.

LeMasters, E. E. (1975). *Blue-collar aristocrats: Life-styles at a working-class tavern*. Madison, WN: University of Wisconsin Press (p. 96).

Masters, W., & Johnson, V. (1970). *Human Sexual Inadequacy*. Boston: Little, Brown.

Rainwater, L. (1964). Marital sexuality in four cultures of poverty. *Journal of Marriage and the Family 26*, 457-466.

Scanzoni, J. (1972). Rethinking Christian perspectives on family planning and population control. *Journal of the American Scientific Affiliation 4*, (supplement No. 1), 2-8.

Wiese, B. R. (1972). *Everything You Need to Know to Stay Married and Like It*. Grand Rapids, Michigan: Zondervan (pp. 100-101).

CHAPTER 6

Blood, R. O., & Wolfe, D. M. (1960) *Husbands and Wives: The Dynamics of Married Living*. New York: The Free Press.

Christenson, L. (1970). *The Christian Family*. Minneapolis, MN: Bethany Fellowship.

Condran, J. G., & Bode, J. G. (1982). Rashomon, working wives, and family division of labor: Middletown, 1980. *Journal of Marriage and the Family 44* (May), 421-426.

Coverman, S., & Sheley, J. F. (1986). Change in men's housework and childcare time, 1965-1975. *Journal of Marriage and the Family 48*, 413-422.

Erickson, J. A., Yancey, W. L., & Erickson, E. (1979). The division of family roles. *Journal of Marriage and the Family 41* (May), 301-313.

Ferber, M. (1982). Labor market participation of young married women: Causes and effects. *Journal of Marriage and the Family 44,* 457-468.

Mackey, W. C. (1985). A cross-cultural perspective on perceptions of paternalistic differences in the United States: The myth of the derelict daddy. *Sex Roles 12* (5/6), 509-533.

Saxton, L. (1980). *The Individual, Marriage and the Family* (4th ed.). Belmont, California: Wadsworth (p. 547).

Scanzoni, L. D., & Scanzoni, J. (1988). *Men, Women, and Change.* New York: McGraw-Hill (pp. 293-296).

Stafford, R., Backman, E., & diBonda, P. (1977). The division of labor among cohabiting and married couples. *Journal of Marriage and the Family 39* (Feb.), 43-57.

Strong, B., DeVault, C., Suid, M., & Reynolds, R. (1983). *The Marriage and Family Experience* (2nd ed.). New York: West Publications (p. 185).

Wiese, B. R., & Steinmetz, U. G. (1972). *Everything You Need to Know to Stay Married and Like It.* Grand Rapids, Michigan: Zondervan (p. 149).

CHAPTER 7

Blood, R. O., Jr. & Wolfe, D. M. (1960). *Husbands and Wives: The Dynamics of Married Living.* New York: The Free Press (p. 253).

Barling, J. (1984). Effects of husbands' work experiences on wives' marital satisfaction. *The Journal of Social Psychology 124,* 219-225.

Campolo, A. (1984, November). *Work with integrity.* Paper presented at the meeting of the Association of Nazarene Sociologists of Religion, Kansas City, MO.

Gaesser, D. L., & Whitbourne, S. K. (1985). Work identity and marital adjustment in blue-collar men. *Journal of Marriage and the Family 47* (3), 747-751.

Greiff, B. S., & Munter, P. K. (1981). *Trade-offs: Executive, Family, and Organizational Life.* New York: Mentor Books.

Homans, G. C. (1961). *Social Behavior: Its Elementary Forms.* New York: Harcourt, Brace, and World.

Seidenberg, R. (1973). *Corporate Wives—Corporate Casualties?* Garden City, NY: Doubleday.

Treisman, D. (1977). *Occupational Prestige in Comparative Perspective.* New York: Academic Press (Table 7.2 and appendix A).

CHAPTER 8

Barnett, R. C., & Baruch, G. K. (1987). Determinants of fathers' participation in family work. *Journal of Marriage and the Family 49*, 29-40.

Booth, A., Johnson, D. R., & White, L. (1984). Women, outside employment, and marital instability. *American Journal of Sociology 90* (3), 567-583.

Campolo, Anthony (1987). *A Straight Word to Kids and Parents*. Ulster Park, NY: Plough Publication House.

Caplow, T., Bahr, H. M., Chadwick, B. A., Hill, R., & Williamson, M. H. (1982). *Middletown Families: Fifty Years of Change and Continuity*. Minneapolis, Minnesota: University of Minnesota Press (p. 99).

Christenson, Larry. (1970). *The Christian Family*. Minneapolis, MN: Bethany Fellowship. (pp. 127-128).

Coverman, S., & Sheley, J. F. (1986). Change in men's housework and child-care time, 1965-1975. *Journal of Marriage and the Family 48*, 413-422.

Hiller, D. V., & Philliber, W. W. (1986). The division of labor in contemporary marriage: Expectations, perceptions, and performance. *Social Problems 33* (3), 191-201.

Johnson, W. R., & Skinner, J. (1986). Labor supply and marital separation. *American Economic Review 76* (3), 455-69.

Mackey, W. C. (1985). A cross-cultural perspective on perceptions of paternalistic deficiencies in the United States: The myth of the derelict daddy. *Sex Roles 12* (5/6), 509-533.

Michael, R. T. (1977). *Why has the U.S. divorce rate doubled within the decade?*. (Working Paper No. 202) National Bureau of Economic Research.

Miller, J., & Garrison, H. H. (1982). Sex roles: The division of labor at home and in the workplace. *Annual Review of Sociology 8*, 237-262.

Moore, K., Spain, D., & Mianchi, S. M. (1984). The working wife and mother. *Marriage and Family Review 7*, 77-98.

Nock, S. L. (1987). *Sociology of the Family*. Englewood Cliffs, NJ: Prentice-Hall (p. 160).

Rapaport, R., & Rapaport, R. N. (1976). *Dual-Career Families Reexamined*. New York: Harper and Row.

Rosenfeld, L. B., & Welsh, S. M. (1985). Differences in self-disclosure in dual-career and single-career marriages. *Communication Monographs 52* (3), 253-263.

Schoen, R., & Urton, W. L. (1979). A theoretical perspective on cohort marriage and divorce in twentieth century Sweden. *Journal of Marriage and the Family 41*, 409-416.

Simpson, I. H., & England, P. (1981). Conjugal work roles and marital solidarity. *Journal of Family Issues 2*, 180-204.

Smith, D. S. (1985). Wife employment and marital adjustment: A cumulation of results. *Family Relations 34*, 483-490.

Spitz, G. (1988). Women's employment and family relations: A review. *Journal of Marriage and the Family 50* (August), 595- 618.

Terry, D. & Scott, W. A. (1987). Gender differences in correlates of marital satisfaction. *Australian Journal of Psychology 39* (2), 207-221.

United States Bureau of the Census. (1983). *Statistical abstract of the United States: 1984* (104th ed.). (USBC Publication No. 683). Washington, D.C.: U.S. Government Printing Office. (p. 413).

Waite, L. (1980). Working wives and the family life cycle. *American Journal of Sociology 86* (2), 272-294.

Wang, B. & Stellway, R. J. (1987). *Should You Be the Working Mom?* Elgin, IL: David C. Cook.

CHAPTER 9

Bellah, R. N., Madsen, R., Sullivan, W. M., Swindler, A., & Tipton, S. M. (1985). *Habits of the Heart: Individualism and Commitment in American Life.* Berkeley: University of California Press (pp. 142-166).

Belsky, J. (1985). Exploring individual differences in marital change across the transition to parenthood: The role of violated expectations. *Journal of Marriage and the Family 47* (4), 1037-1044.

Converse, P., Rogers, W., & Campbell, A. (1975, May). The American way of mating: Marriage si, children only . . . maybe. *Psychology Today*, p. 38.

Gilbert, L, et al. (1982). Perceptions of parental role responsibilities: Differences between mothers and fathers. *Family Relations 31* (April), 261-269.

Harriman, L. (1983). Personal and marital changes accompanying parenthood. *Family Relations 32* (July), 387-394.

Holstege, H. (1982). The Christian family. *Occasional Papers from Calvin College* 2 (1), 20-21.

LaHaye, T. & LaHaye, B. (1976). *The Act of Marriage.* Grand Rapids, MI: Zondervan (p. 185).

LeMasters, E. E. & DeFrain, J. (1983). *Parents in Contemporary America: A Sympathetic View.* Homewood, Illinois: Dorsey.

Overstreet, H. A. (1949). *The Mature Mind.* New York: W.W. Norton.

Scanzoni, J. (1976). Rethinking Christian perspectives on family planning and population control. *Journal of the American Scientific Affiliation (Supplement No. 1)*, 2-8.

Scanzoni, L. D., & Scanzoni, J. (1981). *Men, Women, and Change* (2nd ed.). New York: McGraw-Hill (pp. 513-516).

Toffler, A. (1970). *Future Shock.* New York:Random House (pp. 207-8).

Weiss, R. (1985). Men and the family. *Family Processes 24*, 49-58.

Weitzman, L. (1985). *The Divorce Revolution: The Unexpected Social and Economic Consequences for Women and Children in America.* New York: The Free Press.

Zopf, P. E., Jr. (1984). *Population: An Introduction to Social Demography.* Palo Alto, CA: Mayfield (pp. 15-16; 41- 42).

CHAPTER 10

Balswick, J. O., & Peek, C. W. (1971). The inexpressive male: A tragedy of American society. *The Family Coordinator 20*, 363-368.

Becker, G. (1973). A theory of marriage. *Journal of Political Economy 81*, 813-845.

Bell, R. (1983). *Marriage and Family Interaction 6th ed.*. Homewood, IL: Dorsey.

Boland, J. P., & Follingstad, D. R. (1987). The relation between communication and marital satisfaction: A review. *Journal of Sex and Marital Therapy 13* (4), 286-313.

Brain, R. (1976) *Friends and Lovers*. New York: Basic Books.

Burr, W. R. (1976). *Successful Marriage: A Principles Approach*. Homewood, IL: Dorsey Press.

Cutler, B., & Dyer, W. G. (1971). Initial adjustment processes in young married couples. In J. P. Wiseman (Ed.), *People as Partners* (pp. 184-195). San Francisco: Canfield.

Dating survey rates desired dates. (1976, October 8). *Wheaton College Weekly*, p. 3.

Eshleman, J. R. (1985). *The Family: An Introduction* (4th ed.). Boston: Allyn and Bacon (p. 584).

Fromm, E. (1956). *The Art of Loving: An Inquiry into the Nature of Love*. New York: Harper and Row (pp.29-32).

Goode, W. (1982) *The Family, 2nd ed.* Englewood Cliffs, New Jersey: Prentice-Hall

Hansen, J. E. & Schuldt, W. J. (1984). Marital self-disclosure and marital satisfaction. *Journal of Marriage and the Family 46* (4), 923-926.

Johnson, D. W. (1973). Building self-actualizing relationships. In D. Johnson (Ed.), *Contemporary Social Psychology* (pp. 49-64). New York: J. B. Lippincott.

Kirkpatrik, C. (1963). *The Family*. New York: Ronald.

Komarovsky, M. (1976) Learning conjugal roles. In Jerald Heiss (Ed.), *Family Roles and Interaction, 2nd ed.*. (pp. 58-71). Chicago: Rand McNally.

Knox, D. (1985). *Choices in Relationships*. New York: West Publishing.

Mace, D., & Mace, V. (1960). *Marriage East and West*. Garden City, New York: Doubleday.

Murstein, B. I. (1970). Stimulus-value-role: A theory of marital choice. *Journal of Marriage and the Family 32*, 465-481.

Richman, J. (1977). Bargaining for sex and status: The dating service and sex-role change. In P. J. Stein, J. Richman, & N. Hannon (Eds.), *The family: Functions, Conflicts, and Symbols* (pp. 158-165). Reading, Massachusetts: Addison-Wesley.

Rubin, Z. (1973). *Liking and Loving*. New York: Holt.

Safian, L. J. (1966). *An Irreverant Dictionary of Love and Marriage*. New York: Belmont (p. 84).

Sporakowski, M. J., & Hughston, G. A. (1978). Prescriptions for happy marriage: Adjustments and satisfactions of couples married fifty years or more. *Family Coordinator 27*, 321-327.

Stinnett, N., Walters, J., & Kaye, E. (1984). *Relations in Marriage and the Family, 2nd ed.* New York: Macmillan.

Yelsma, P. & Athappilly, K. (1988). Marital satisfaction and communication practices: Comparisons among Indian and American couples. *Journal of Comparative Family Studies 19* (1), 37-54.

CHAPTER 11

Burgess, E. W., Locke, H. J., & Thomas, M. M. (1971). *The Family: From Tradition to Companionship*, 4th ed. New York: Van Nostrand Reinhold (p. 351).

Burr, W. R. (1976) *Successful Marriage: A Principles Approach*. Homewood, IL: The Dorsey Press (pp. 240-41).

Christenson, L. (1970). *The Christian Family*. Minneapolis, MN: Bethany Fellowship (pp.32-54).

DeJong, G., & Wilson, D. R. (1979). *Husband and Wife*. Grand Rapids, MI: Zondervan.

Elliot, E. (1989). Femininity: What women were made for. *Transformation: An International Dialogue on Evangelical Social Ethics 6* (2), 26.

Graham, R. (1975). Comment in "Others Say . . ." column. *Christianity Today*, June 6, p. 32.

Gundry, P. (1980). *Heirs Together: Mutual Submission in Marriage*. Grand Rapids, Michigan: Zondervan (p. 24).

Gunther, R. (1976, August) *Androgyny*. Paper presented at the 29th annual American Institute of Family Relations Workshop, Long Beach, CA.

Hiller, D. V. & Philliber, W. W. (1986). The division of labor in contemporary marriage: Expectations, perceptions, and performance. *Social Problems 33* (3), 191-201.

Jewett, P. K. (1975). *Man as Male and Female*. Grand Rapids, Michigan: Eerdmans.

Krausz, S. L. (1986). Sex roles within marriage. *Social Work 31* (6), 457-464.

Kraybill, D. B. (1980). Jesus and the stigmatized: A sociological analysis of the four gospels. In C. P. DeSanto, C. Redekop, W. L. Smith-Hinds (Eds.). *A Reader in Sociology: Christian Perspectives* (pp. 399-413). Scottdale, PA: Herald Press.

LaHaye, T. & LaHaye, B. (1976). *The Act of Marriage*. Grand Rapids, Michigan: Zondervan.

Levande, D. I., Koch, J. B., & Koch, L. Z. (1983). *Marriage and the Family*. Boston: Houghton Mifflin (pp. 468-9).

Lynd, R. S. & Lynd, H. M. (1929) *Middletown*. New York: Harcourt, Brace, and World.

Lynd, R. S., & Lynd, H. M. (1937) *Middletown in Transition*. New York: Harcourt, Brace, and World.

Parsons, T. & Bales, R. F. (1955). *Family, Socialization and Interaction Process*. Glencoe, Illinois: The Free Press.

Pleck, J. H. (1979). Men's family work: Three perspectives and some new data. *The Family Coordinator 28 (4)*, 481-488.

Regan, M. C., & Roland, H. E. (1985). Rearranging family and career priorities: Professional women and men of the eighties. *Journal of Marriage and the Family 47* (4), 985-992.

Scanzoni, J. (1979). *Love and Negotiate: Creative Conflict in Marriage*. Waco, TX: Word Press.

Szinovacs, M. E. (1984). Changing family roles and interactions. *Marriage and Family Review 7* (3,4), 163-201.

Weeks, J. (1989). *Population: An Introduction to Concepts and Issues* (4th ed.) Belmont, CA, Wadsworth.

CHAPTER 12

Bibby, R. W., & Brinkerhoff, M. B. (1973). Why conservative churches are growing: Kelley revisited. *Journal for the scientific study of religion* (September), 273-283.

Blood, R. O., & Wolfe, D. M. (1960). *Husbands & Wives: The Dynamics of Married Living*. New York: Free Press.

Burgess, E. W., Locke, H. J., & Thomas, M. M. (1971). *The Family: From Tradition to Companionship*. New York: Van Nostrand.

Crow, K. (1986, March 20-22). *Economic beliefs and compassionate ministry in a holiness denomination*. Paper presented at the 5th annual meeting of the Association of Nazarene Sociologists of Religion, Kansas City, Missouri.

Komarovsky, M. (1962). *Blue-collar Marriage*. New York: Random House.

Lynd, R. S., & Lund, H. M. (1929). *Middletown: A Study in Contemporary Culture*. New York: Harcourt, Brace.

Lynd, R. S., & Lynd, H. M. (1937). *Middletown in Transition: A Study in Cultural Conflicts*. New York: Harcourt, Brace & World.

McNamara, R. (1984). Conservative Christian families and their moral world: Some reflections for sociologists. *Sociological Analysis 46* (2), 93-99.

Appendix

TABLE A.1. Total family income of Christiantown respondents

==

Annual Income (in dollars)	percentage of families
10,000 to 14,999	04
15,000 to 19,999	05
20,000 to 24,999	18
25,000 to 29,999	19
30,000 or 39,999	28
40,000 or more	26
total	100%

TABLE A.2.* Frequency of church attendance and rating of marital happiness

==

Church Attendance (number)	Percent rating their marriage "very happy"
At least once per week (n=122)	78.7%
About once per week to once per month (n=105)	57.2%
Less often or never (n=121)	88.5%

Kurskal-Wallis H = 30.71; p = ≤ .001
*1987 General Social Sruvey; white married parents between 25 and 55 years of age

TABLE A.3.* Frequency of prayer and rating of marital happiness

```
================================================================
```

Prayer (number)	Percent rating their marriage "very happy"
More than once per day (n=91)	72.5%
Daily (n=124)	65.3%
Weekly to several times per week (n=109)	56.0%
Less than once per week (n=52)	58.4%

Kruskal-Wallis H = 6.92; p = ≤.08
*General Social Survey; white, married parents between 25 and 55 years of age

TABLE A.4.* Total family income and rating of marital happiness

===

Income (1986)	Percent rating their marriage "very happy"	
	Wives (number)	Husbands (number)
Less than $30,000	45.7% (n=70)	69.2% (n=65)
$30,000 to < $40,000	62.5% (n=40)	66.7% (n=39)
$40,000 to < $50,000	78.6% (n=28)	67.9% (n=28)
$ >50,000	65.2% (n=46)	57.4% (n=54)

Kruskal-Wallis H for wives = 10.44; p = ⩽.05
Kruskal-Wallis H for husbands = 2.02; p = ⩽.57
*1987 General Social Survey; white, married women between 25 and 55 years of age

TABLE A.5. Religious group affiliation of Christiantowners

==

Group/Denomination	Number
Catholic	17
Presbyterian	14
Methodist	8
Baptist	11
Lutheran	15
Episcopal	2
Unitarian	2
Independent/Nondenoml	19
Christian/Undesignated	3
No preference	1
Agnostic	1
Other	2

Total	95

TABLE A.6. Religious orthodoxy index

===

Respondents were given one point for each of the following statements they agreed with:

1. I know God really exists and I have no doubts about it.

2. Jesus is the Divine Son of God and I have no doubts about it.

3. Some men will live forever with God in Heaven.

4. The Bible is completely consistent and without error.

TABLE A.7. Items incorporated in the Locke-Wallace Marital Adjustment Scale

----

```
 1. Marital happiness (self rating)
 2. Agreement of handling family finances
 3. Agreement on matters of recreation
 4. Agreement on demonstrations of affection
 5. Agreement on friends
 6. Agreement on sex relations
 7. Agreement on matters of conventionality
 8. Agreement on philosophy of life
 9. Agreement on ways of dealing with in-laws
10. Democratic means of settling disagreements
11. Mutuality of outside interests
12. Agreement on spending leisure time at home
13. * Absence of consideration of separation
14. Selection of present spouse if life could be lived over
15. Frequency of confiding with mate
```

----

*This item was substituted for an original item which asked whether the respondent had ever wished he/she had not married. Since this wish could have been expressed in response to item 14, the original item 13 was redundant and therefore replaced.

FIGURE A.1.* Employment status of wife, work satisfaction, and rating of marital happiness

```
==================================================================

Employment Status &        Percent Rating their Marriage
  Job Satisfaction                "Very Happy"
    (number)
------------------------------------------------------------------


Full-time
 housewife
  (n=116)        *********************** 58.6%

Working/very
 satisfied w/ job
  (n=44)         ******************************************** 79.5%

Working/dissatisfied to
 moderately satisfied w/ job
  (n=44)         ************************** 52.3%

------------------------------------------------------------------
```

Kruskal-Wallis H = 6.05; p = .01
*1987 General Social Survey; white married women between 25 and 55 years of age

FIGURE A.2.* Theological self-designation and average number of children

```
=========================================================
    Theology            Average Number of Children
    (number)
---------------------------------------------------------


Fundamentalist
    (n=153)       ************************* 2.39

Moderate
    (n=188)       *********************** 2.27

Liberal
    (n=138)       ***************** 1.79

---------------------------------------------------------
```

Pearson product moment correlation = $-.16$, p = ≤ .001
*1987 General Social Survey; white, married parents between 20 and 50 years of age

Index